A-Z TUNBRIDGE WELLS SEVENOAKS

G000298236

CONTENTS

REFERENCE

Motorway	**M25**
A Road	A264
B Road	B2169
Dual Carriageway	
One-way Street — Traffic flow on A Roads is also indicated by a heavy line on the driver's left.	
Road Under Construction — Opening dates are correct at the time of publication.	
Proposed	
Restricted Access	
Pedestrianized Road	
Track / Footpath	
Residential Walkway	
Railway	Level Crossing — Station — Tunnel
Heritage Railway & Station	
Built-up Area	YORK RD.
Local Authority Boundary	
Posttown Boundary	
Postcode Boundary (within Posttown)	
Map Continuation	**5** — Large Scale Centre **40**

Car Park (selected)	P
Church or Chapel	†
Cycleway (selected)	
Fire Station	■
Hospital	H
House Numbers (A & B Roads only)	145 98
Information Centre	i
National Grid Reference	555
Police Station	▲
Post Office	★
Safety Camera with Speed Limit — Fixed cameras and long term road works cameras. Symbols do not indicate camera direction.	(30) Fixed Speed Limit
Toilet: without facilities for the Disabled	▽
with facilities for the Disabled	▽
Disabled use only	▽
Educational Establishment	▭
Hospital or Healthcare Building	▭
Industrial Building	▭
Leisure or Recreational Facility	▭
Place of Interest	▭
Public Building	▭
Shopping Centre or Market	▭
Other Selected Buildings	▭

SCALE

Map Pages 2-39   1:19000   3.33 inches to 1 mile

0   ¼   ½ Mile

0   250   500   750 Metres
5.26cm to 1km   8.47cm to 1 mile

Map Page 40   1:9500   6.7 inches to 1 mile

0   ⅛   ¼ Mile

0   125   250   375 Metres
10.53cm to 1km   16.94cm to 1 mile

Copyright of Geographers' A-Z Map Company Limited

Fairfield Road, Borough Green, Sevenoaks, Kent TN15 8PP
Telephone: 01732 781000 (Enquiries & Trade Sales)
           01732 783422 (Retail Sales)

www.az.co.uk

Copyright © Geographers' A-Z Map Co. Ltd.

Edition 4 2012

 Ordnance Survey This product includes mapping data licensed from Ordnance Survey® with the permission of the Controller of Her Majesty's Stationery Office.

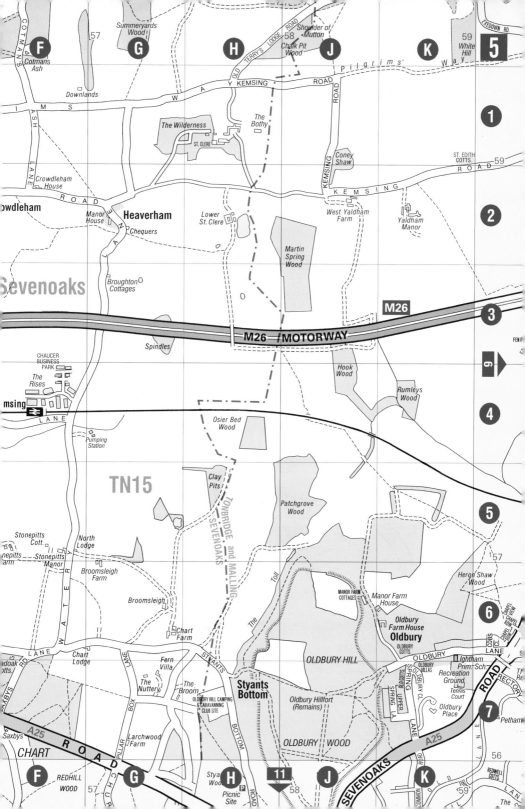

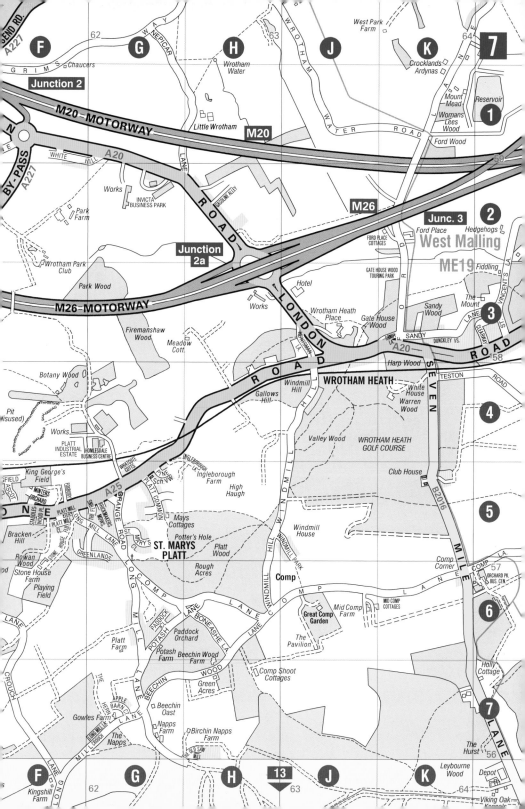

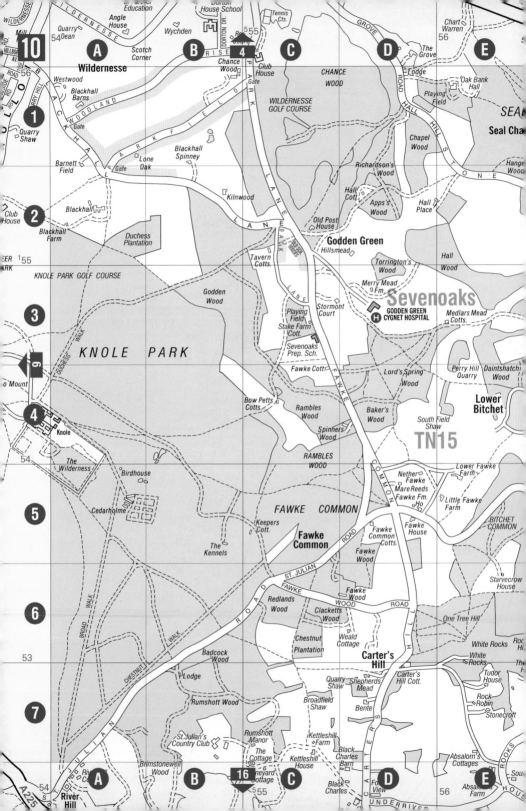

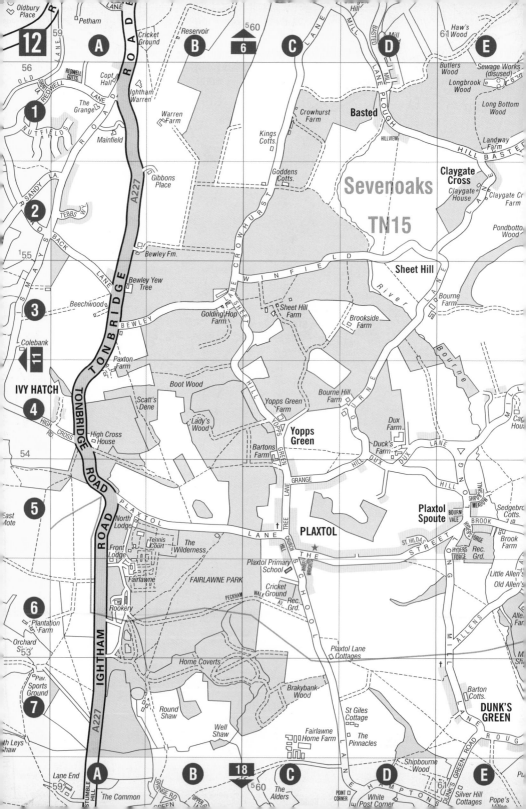

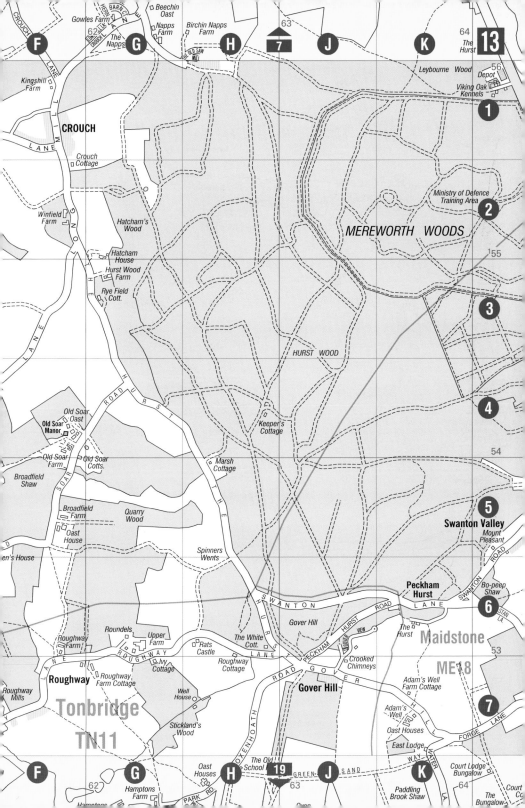

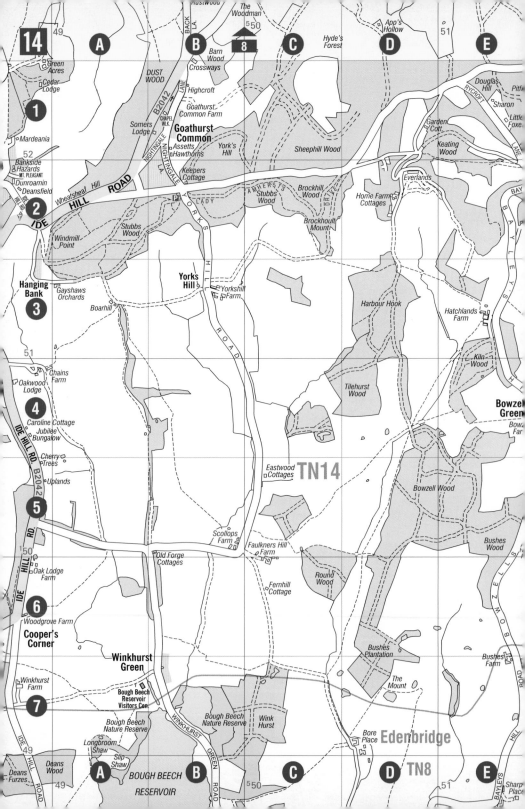

14

49 · A · B · 8 · C · Hyde's Forest · D · App's Hollow · 51 · E

Green Acres · Cedar Lodge · DUST WOOD · B2042 · The Woodman · 550 · Barn Wood · Crossways · Highcroft · Goathurst Common Farm · Douglas Hill · RYCROFT · Pitfi · Sharon · Little Foxe

1

Mardeania · 52 · Bankside & Hazards · MT. PLEASANT · Dunroamin · Deansfield · HILL RD. · Wheatsheaf Hill · HILL · ROAD · Somers Lodge · NIGHTINGALE · NIGHTINGALE LA. · CHAPEL WLK. · **Goathurst Common** · Assetts · Hawthorns · York's Hill · Keepers Cottage · Sheephill Wood · Garden Cott. · Keating Wood · Everlands · BAYLEY'S · LANE

2

IDE · Windmill Point · Stubbs Wood · YORKS · HILL · LADY · AMHERSTS · Stubbs Wood · Brockhill Wood · Brockhoult Mount · Home Farm Cottages

3

Hanging Bank · Gayshaws Orchards · Boarhill · ROAD · **Yorks Hill** · Yorkshill Farm · Harbour Hook · Hatchlands Farm · Kiln Wood · BAY

51

4

Chains Farm · Oakwood Lodge · IDE HILL RD. · Caroline Cottage · Jubilee Bungalow · B2042 · Cherry Trees · Uplands · Tilehurst Wood · Bowzel Green · Bowz. Far

5

150 · HILL · RD. · Eastwood Cottages · **TN14** · Bowzell Wood · Bushes Wood

6

IDE · Oak Lodge Farm · Scollops Farm · Faulkners Hill Farm · Old Forge Cottages · Fernhill Cottage · Round Wood · WOBZELLS · ROAD

Woodgrove Farm · Cooper's Corner · Bushes Plantation · Bushes Farm

7

Winkhurst Farm · **Winkhurst Green** · Bough Beech Reservoir Visitors Cen · WINKHURST · GREEN ROAD · Bough Beech Nature Reserve · Wink Hurst · The Mount · Bore Place · **Edenbridge** · HILL

49 · Deans Wood · Deans Furzes · IDE HILL ROAD · 49 · Longbroom Shaw · Slip Shaw · **BOUGH BEECH** · **RESERVOIR** · 550 · **TN8** · 51 · Sharp Place · BAYLEYS

A · B · C · D · E

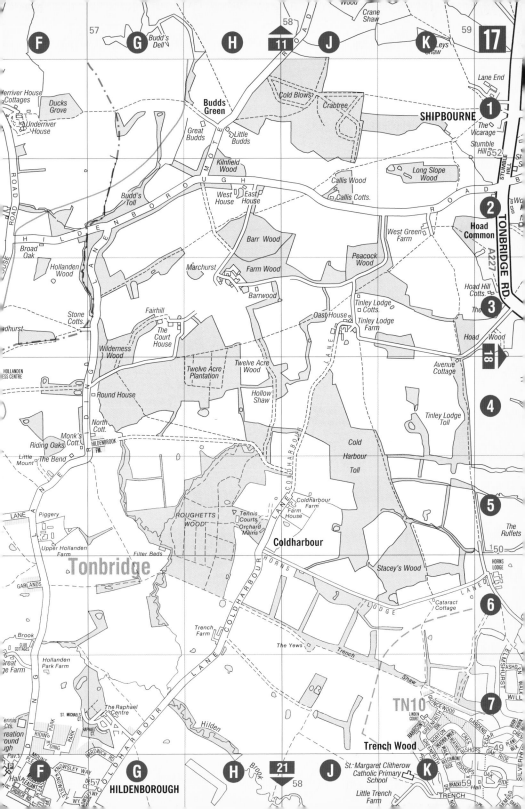

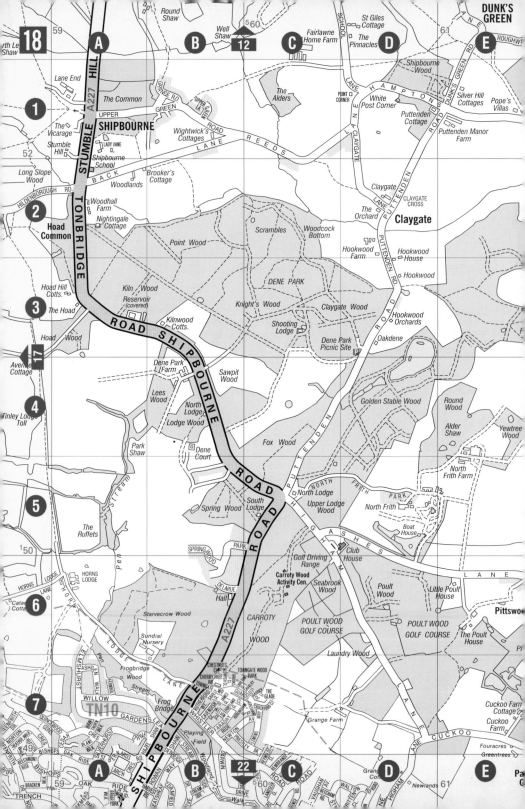

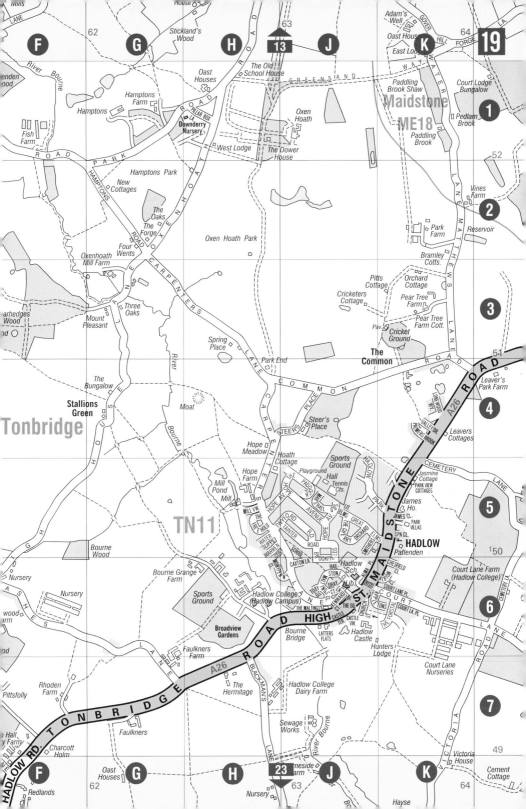

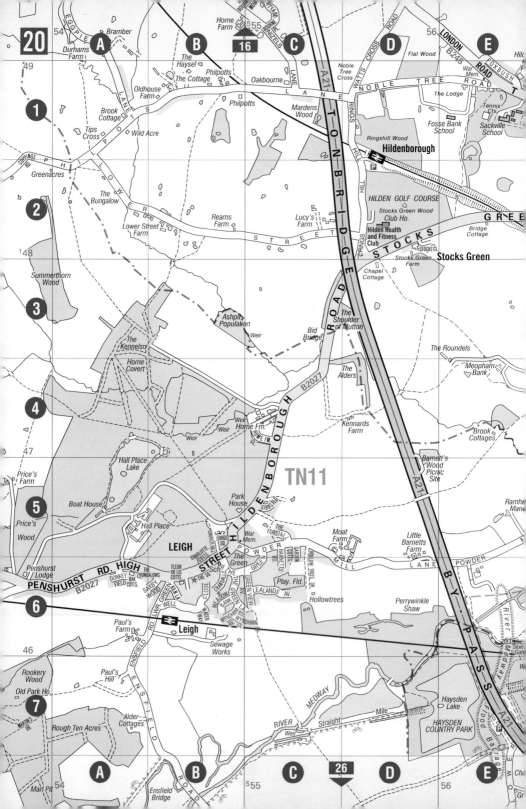

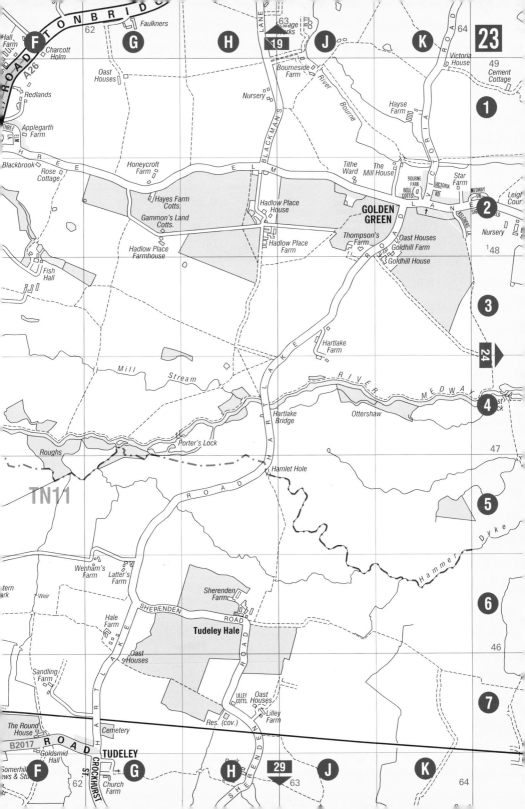

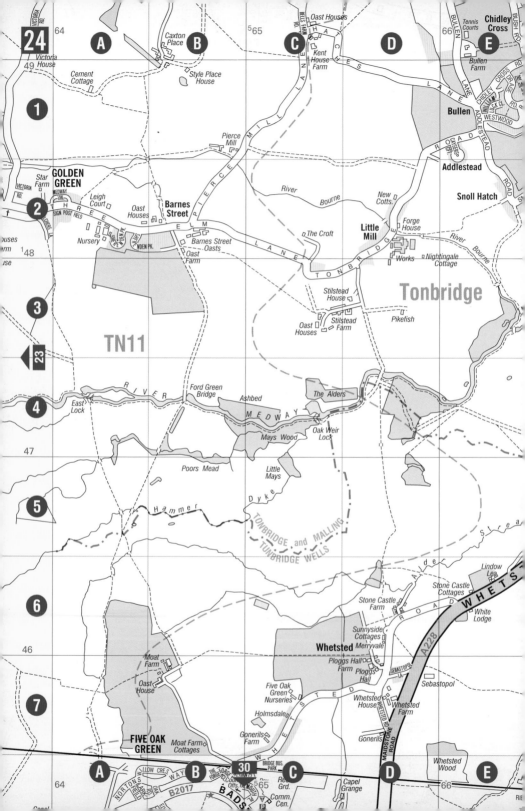

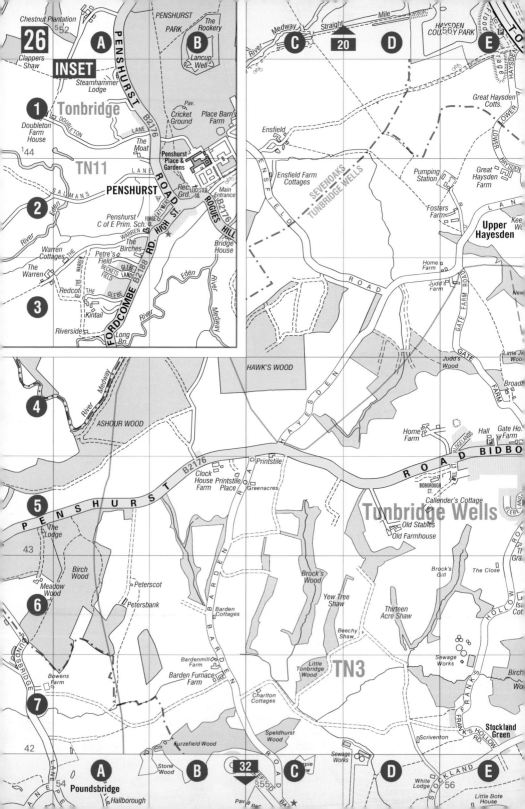

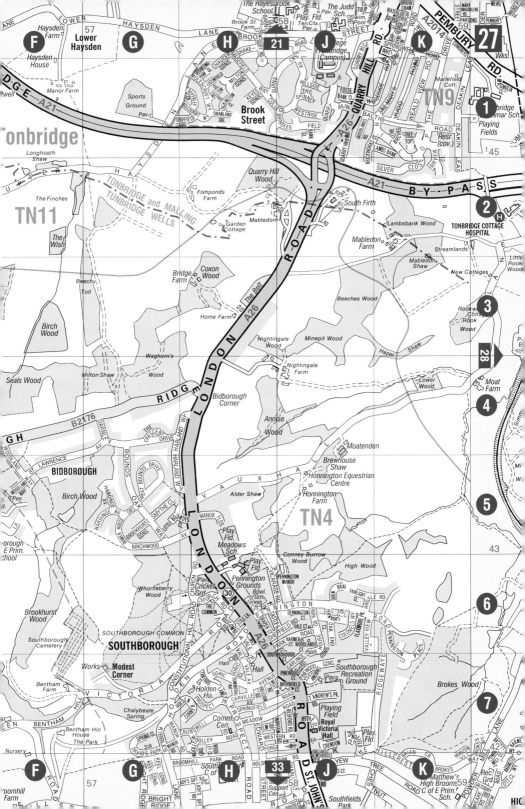

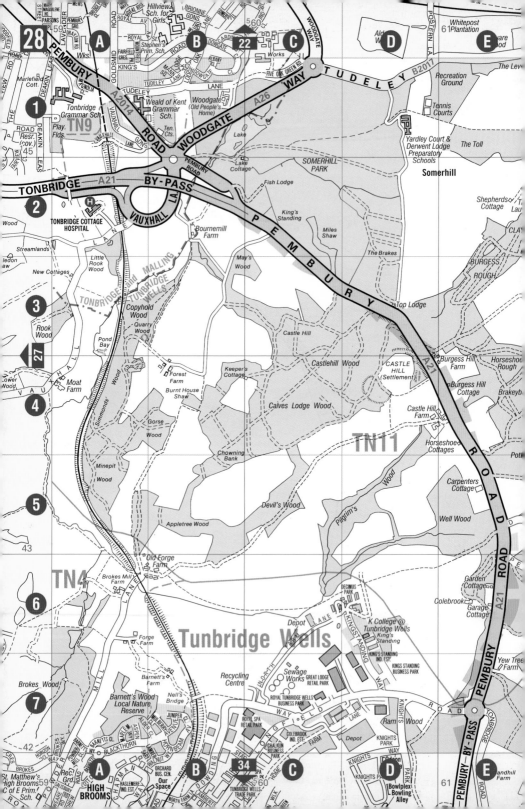

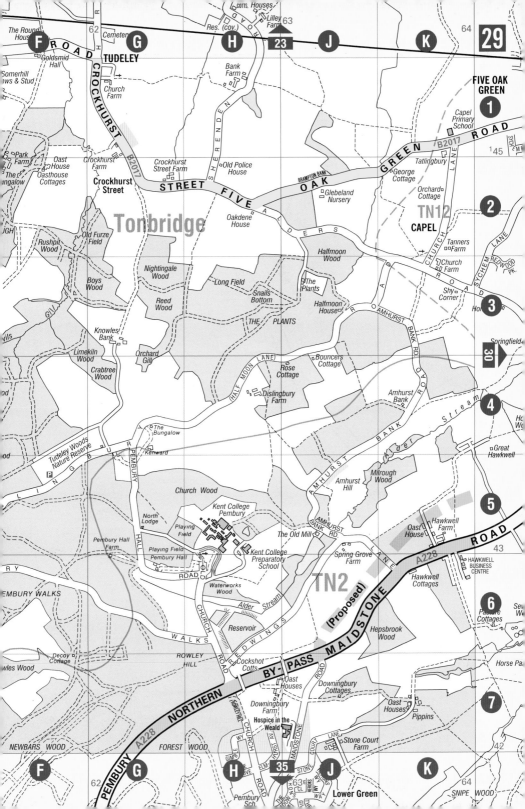

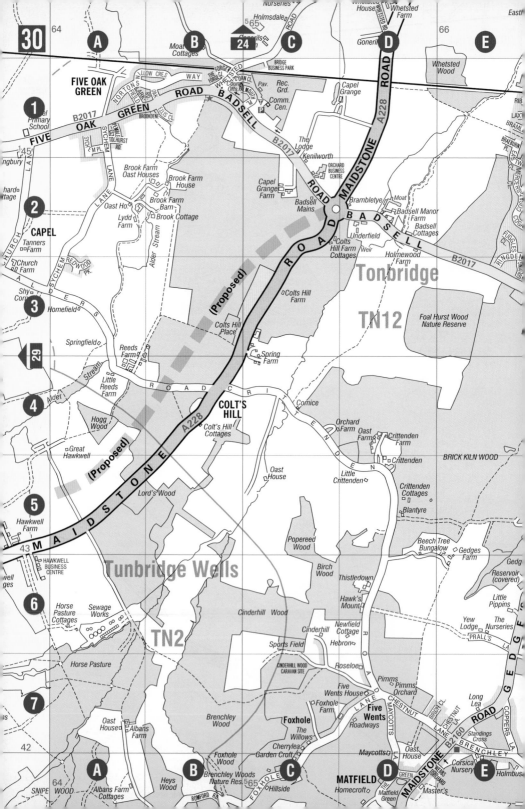

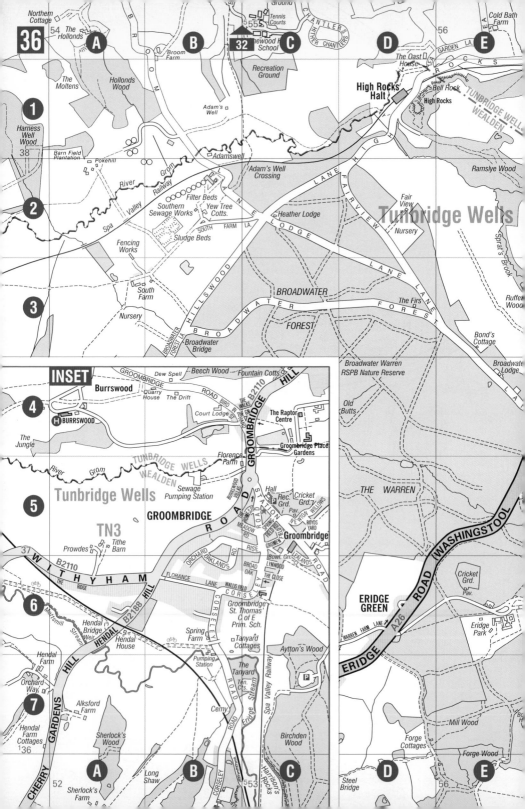

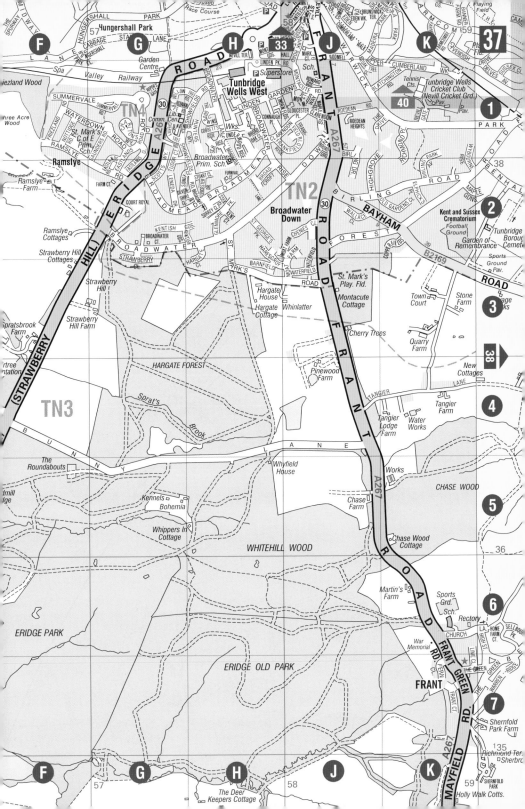

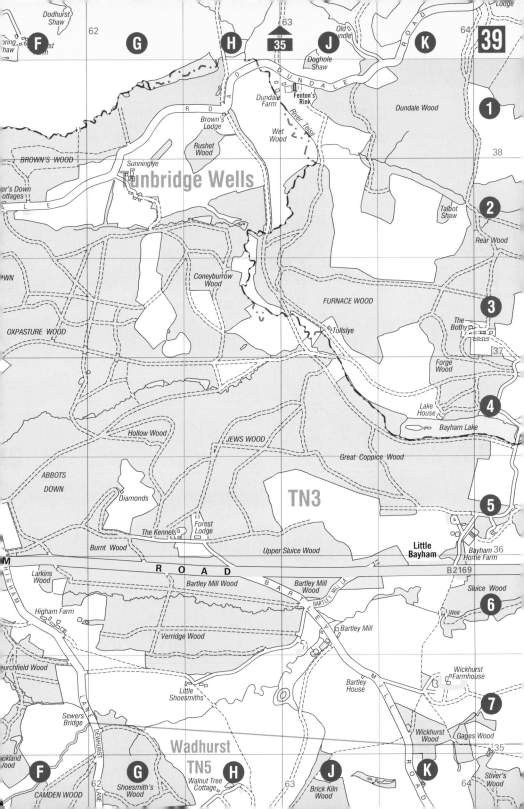

F 62 G H 35 J K 64 K

Dodhurst Shaw
spring haw
st rm
Lodge
Old Dundle
Doghole Shaw

1 Dundale Wood

DUNDALE ROAD

Dundale Farm
Fenton's Rink
River Teise
Wet Wood
Brown's Lodge
Rushet Wood

BROWN'S WOOD

Sunninglye

Tunbridge Wells

er's Down ottages

38

2 Talbot Shaw
Rear Wood

WN

Coneyburrow Wood

FURNACE WOOD

3 The Bothy

OXPASTURE WOOD

Tollslye

37

Forge Wood

4 Lake House
Bayham Lake

Hollow Wood

JEWS WOOD

Great Coppice Wood

ABBOTS DOWN

TN3

Diamonds

5

The Kennels
Forest Lodge

Little Bayham
Bayham 36
Home Farm

Burnt Wood
Upper Sluice Wood

B2169

Larkins Wood

R O A D

Bartley Mill Wood
Bartley Mill Wood

Sluice Wood

6 Weir

Higham Farm

BARTLEY MILL LA

Verridge Wood

Bartley Mill

urchfield Wood

Wickhurst Farmhouse

Little Shoesmiths

Bartley House

7

Sewers Bridge

MILL ROAD

Wickhurst Wood
Gages Wood

Wadhurst

TN5

135

F 62 G H 63 J K 64 K

okland ood
CAMDEN WOOD

DEWHURST LANE

Shoesmith's Wood
Walnut Tree Cottage
Brick Kiln Wood
Stiver's Wood

INDEX

Including Streets, Places & Areas, Hospitals etc., Industrial Estates,
Selected Flats & Walkways, Stations and Selected Places of Interest.

HOW TO USE THIS INDEX

1. Each street name is followed by its Postcode District, then by its Locality abbreviation(s) and then by its map reference;
   e.g. **Addlestead Rd.** TN12: E Peck . . . .1E **24** is in the TN12 Postcode District and the East Peckham Locality and is to be found in square 1E on page **24**. The page number is shown in bold type.

2. A strict alphabetical order is followed in which Av., Rd., St., etc. (though abbreviated) are read in full and as part of the street name;
   e.g. **Greenview Cres.** appears after **Green Vw. Av.** but before **Green Way**

3. Streets and a selection of flats and walkways that cannot be shown on the mapping, appear in the index with the thoroughfare to which they are connected shown in brackets; e.g. **Albion M.** TN1: Tun W . . . .4A **34** (off Albion Rd.)

4. Addresses that are in more than one part are referred to as not continuous.

5. Places and areas are shown in the index in **BLUE TYPE** and the map reference is to the actual map square in which the town centre or area is located and not to the place name shown on the map; e.g. **ADDLESTEAD** 1E **24**

6. An example of a selected place of interest is Salomons Mus. 1F **33**

7. An example of a station is **Bat & Ball Station (Rail)** 6J **3**

8. An example of a Hospital, Hospice or selected Healthcare facility is GODDEN GREEN CYGNET HOSPITAL 3D **10**

9. Map references for entries that appear on large scale page **40** are shown first, with small scale map references shown in brackets;
   e.g. **Abbey Ct.** TN4: Tun W 1B **40** (4J **33**)

GENERAL ABBREVIATIONS

All. : Alley	**Flds.** : Fields	**Pde.** : Parade
App. : Approach	**Gdn.** : Garden	**Pk.** : Park
Arc. : Arcade	**Gdns.** : Gardens	**Pas.** : Passage
Av. : Avenue	**Ga.** : Gate	**Pl.** : Place
Bri. : Bridge	**Gt.** : Great	**Ri.** : Rise
Bus. : Business	**Grn.** : Green	**Rd.** : Road
Cvn. : Caravan	**Gro.** : Grove	**Sq.** : Square
Cen. : Centre	**Hgts.** : Heights	**Sta.** : Station
Chu. : Church	**Ho.** : House	**St.** : Street
Cl. : Close	**Ind.** : Industrial	**Ter.** : Terrace
Comn. : Common	**Info.** : Information	**Trad.** : Trading
Cnr. : Corner	**La.** : Lane	**Up.** : Upper
Cott. : Cottage	**Lit.** : Little	**Va.** : Vale
Cotts. : Cottages	**Lwr.** : Lower	**Vw.** : View
Ct. : Court	**Mnr.** : Manor	**Vs.** : Villas
Cres. : Crescent	**Mans.** : Mansions	**Vis.** : Visitors
Cft. : Croft	**Mdw.** : Meadow	**Wlk.** : Walk
Dr. : Drive	**Mdws.** : Meadows	**W.** : West
E. : East	**M.** : Mews	**Yd.** : Yard
Ent. : Enterprise	**Mt.** : Mount	
Est. : Estate	**Mus.** : Museum	
Fld. : Field	**Nth.** : North	

LOCALITY ABBREVIATIONS

Addtn : **Addington**	Hdlw : **Hadlow**	Rough : **Roughway**
Bell G : **Bell's Yew Green**	Hals : **Halstead**	R'hall : **Rusthall**
Bess G : **Bessels Green**	Hild : **Hildenborough**	Seal : **Seal**
Bidb : **Bidborough**	Ide H : **Ide Hill**	S'oaks : **Sevenoaks**
Bor G : **Borough Green**	Igh : **Ightham**	S'brne : **Shipbourne**
Bou B : **Bough Beech**	Ivy H : **Ivy Hatch**	S'bgh : **Southborough**
Brenc : **Brenchley**	Kems'g : **Kemsing**	Speld : **Speldhurst**
Cap : **Capel**	Knat : **Knatts Valley**	Sund : **Sundridge**
Chev : **Chevening**	Ladd : **Laddingford**	Tonb : **Tonbridge**
Chip : **Chipstead**	Lamb : **Lamberhurst**	Tros : **Trottiscliffe**
Col H : **Colt's Hill**	Lang G : **Langton Green**	Tude : **Tudeley**
Cous W : **Cousley Wood**	Leigh : **Leigh**	Tun W : **Tunbridge Wells**
Crouc : **Crouch**	Mat : **Matfield**	Under : **Underriver**
Dunk G : **Dunk's Green**	Mere : **Mereworth**	Wadh : **Wadhurst**
Dun G : **Dunton Green**	Off : **Offham**	Weald : **Weald**
E Peck : **East Peckham**	Ott : **Otford**	W King : **West Kingsdown**
Eri G : **Eridge Green**	Pad W : **Paddock Wood**	W Peck : **West Peckham**
Five G : **Five Oak Green**	Pem : **Pembury**	Wro : **Wrotham**
Frant : **Frant**	Pens : **Penshurst**	Wro H : **Wrotham Heath**
God G : **Godden Green**	Platt : **Platt**	Yald : **Yalding**
Gold G : **Golden Green**	Plax : **Plaxtol**	
Groom : **Groombridge**	Riv : **Riverhead**	

A

Abbey Ct. TN4: Tun W 1B **40** (4J 33)
Abbott Rd. TN15: Bor G 5D **6**
Acer Av. TN2: Tun W 2A **38**
Acorn Cl. TN12: Five G 1B **30**
Acorns, The TN13: S'oaks 1G **9**
Addison Rd. TN2: Tun W 2A **34**
ADDLESTEAD 1E **24**
Addlestead Rd. TN12: E Peck 1E **24**
Aisher Way TN13: Riv 6E **2**
Akehurst La. TN13: S'oaks 3J **9**
Albany Cl. TN9: Tonb 1B **28**
Albany Hill TN2: Tun W 4A **34**
Albert Cotts. TN1: Tun W 1D **40** (5A 34)
Albert Ct. TN2: Tun W 5B **34**
Albert Rd. TN9: Tonb 6K **21**
Albert St. TN1: Tun W 1C **40** (5K 33)
Albion Cl. TN11: Hdlw 6K **19**
Albion M. TN1: Tun W 4A **34**
(off Albion Rd.)
Albion Rd. TN1: Tun W 4K **33**
Alder Cl. TN4: S'bgh 7A **28**
Alders Mdw. TN9: Tonb 5H **21**
Alders Rd. TN11: Five G, Tude 2H **29**
TN12: Cap 2H **29**
Aldwych Cl. TN10: Tonb 7B **18**
Alexander Ct. TN1: Tun W 2B **40**
Alexandra Rd. TN9: Tonb 7K **21**
Allan Cl. TN4: R'hall 5E **32**
Allandale Rd. TN2: Tun W 3B **34**
Allens La. TN15: Plax 6E **12**
Alliance Way TN12: Pad W 2F **31**
Allington Dr. TN10: Tonb 2E **22**
Allington Rd. TN12: Pad W 1F **31**
Allotment La. TN13: S'oaks 7J **3**
All Saints Ri. TN4: Tun W 3J **33**
All Saints Rd. TN4: Tun W 3J **33**
Alma Pl. TN11: Hdlw 6J **19**
Amberleaze Dr. TN2: Pem 3H **35**
Amberley Cl. TN9: Tonb 7J **21**
Amberley Ct. TN4: Tun W 1A **34**
Amherst Hill TN13: Riv 1F **9**
Amherst Pl. TN13: Riv 7F **3**
Amherst Rd. TN4: Tun W 4J **33**
TN13: S'oaks 7H **3**
Amhurst Bank Rd. TN2: Pem 5J **29**
TN11: Cap 3K **29**
Anchorage Flats TN12: Pad W 2G **31**
Andrew Rd. TN4: Tun W 1A **34**
Andrews Cl. TN2: Tun W 4B **34**
Angel Cen. 6A **22**
Angel Indoor Bowls Cen. 6A **22**
Angel La. TN9: Tonb 6K **21**
Angel Wlk. TN9: Tonb 6K **21**
Annetts Hall TN15: Bor G 4E **6**
Annison St. TN9: Tonb 5K **21**
Anthony Cl. TN13: Dun G 5E **2**
Apple Barn Ct. TN15: Crouc 7G **7**
Apple Ct. TN12: Pad W 2F **31**
Appletons TN11: Hdlw 6J **19**
Apple Tree La. TN2: Tun W 1B **34**
Apsley St. TN4: R'hall 5F **33**
Archers Pk. TN12: E Peck 2G **25**
Argyle Rd. TN4: S'bgh 6J **27**
TN13: S'oaks 3H **9**
Armstrong Cl. TN14: Hals 1B **2**
Arne Cl. TN10: Tonb 1C **22**
Arnold Bus. Park, The TN12: E Peck ...2G **25**
Arnold's Ct. TN10: Tonb 2A **22**
Arundel Cl. TN9: Tonb 7J **21**
Arundel Rd. TN1: Tun W 5C **40** (7K 33)
Ascot Cl. TN15: Bor G 5F **7**
Ashbourne Pl. TN11: Hild 5B **16**
Ashburnham Cl. TN13: S'oaks 5J **9**
Ashburnham Rd. TN10: Tonb 4A **22**
Ash Cl. TN2: Tun W 2B **38**
Ashcroft Rd. TN12: Pad W 3F **31**
Ashden Wlk. TN10: Tonb 7A **18**

Ashdown Cl. TN4: Tun W 5H **33**
Ashenden Wlk. TN2: Tun W 1C **34**
Asher Reeds TN3: Lang G 5C **32**
Ashes La. TN11: Hdlw 5D **18**
Ashgrove Rd. TN13: S'oaks 5G **9**
Ashley Cl. TN13: S'oaks 2H **9**
Ashley Gdns. TN4: R'hall 5E **32**
Ashley Pk. TN4: R'hall 4E **32**
Ashley Pk. Cl. TN4: R'hall 4E **32**
Ashley Rd. TN11: Hild 2G **21**
TN13: S'oaks 2H **9**
Ash Platt, The TN15: Seal 5A **4**
Ash Platt Rd. TN15: Seal 6A **4**
Aspen Way TN4: S'bgh 7A **28**
Assembly Hall Theatre 3C **40** (5K 33)
Athill Ct. TN13: S'oaks 7J **3**
Auckland Rd. TN1: Tun W 3A **34**
Audley Av. TN9: Tonb 5H **21**
Audley Ri. TN9: Tonb 6H **21**
Audrey Sturley Ct. TN4: R'hall 4F **33**
Aultmore Ct. TN2: Tun W 6A **34**
Avebury Av. TN9: Tonb 6K **21**
Avenue, The TN9: Tonb 5K **21**
TN15: Bor G 4E **6**
Avenue Du Puy TN9: Tonb 6A **22**
Avenue Rd. TN13: S'oaks 2J **9**
Avon Cl. TN10: Tonb 2A **22**
Avon St. TN1: Tun W 4A **34**

B

Back La. TN11: S'brne 2A **18**
TN13: Bess G 7B **8**
TN14: Ide H 7B **8**
TN15: God G 2C **10**
TN15: Igh 2A **12**
Baden Powell Rd. TN13: Riv 6E **2**
Badgers Holt TN2: Tun W 4C **34**
Badsell Rd. TN12: Five G, Pad W 1B **30**
Baldwins La. TN4: Tun W 1A **34**
Ballard Way TN12: Pad W 1H **31**
Balmoral Ho. TN1: Tun W 3A **40**
Baltic Ho. TN1: Tun W 1D **40**
Baltic Rd. TN9: Tonb 1J **27**
Bancroft Rd. TN15: Wro 1D **6**
Bank La. TN11: Hild 4C **16**
TN15: Under 4C **16**
Bankside TN13: Dun G 6D **2**
Bank St. TN9: Tonb 5K **21**
TN13: S'oaks 3J **9**
Banner Farm Rd.
TN2: Tun W 6D **40** (7K 33)
Barchester Way TN10: Tonb 1D **22**
Barclay Av. TN10: Tonb 2D **22**
Barclay Fld. TN15: Kems'g 2A **4**
BARDEN PARK 6H **21**
Barden Pk. Rd. TN9: Tonb 6J **21**
Barden Rd. TN3: Bidb, Speld 6B **26**
TN9: Tonb 6J **21**
BARNES STREET 2B **24**
Barnetts Cl. TN4: S'bgh 7A **28**
Barnetts Rd. TN11: Leigh 5C **20**
Barnetts Way TN4: S'bgh 7A **28**
Barnett's Wood Local Nature Reserve
......................................7A **28**
Barnfield TN2: Tun W 3H **37**
Barnfield Cres. TN15: Kems'g 2A **4**
Barnfield Rd. TN13: Riv 1E **8**
Barons Ct. TN4: Tun W 4J **33**
Barretts Rd. TN13: Dun G 5D **2**
Barrow La. TN3: Lang G 7B **32**
Bartley Mill La. TN3: Lamb 6J **39**
Bartley Mill Rd. TN3: Lamb 6J **39**
TN5: Cous W, Wadh 6J **39**
BASTED 1D **12**
Basted La. TN15: Crouc 1E **12**
Basted Mill TN15: Bor G 6C **6**
BAT & BALL 6J **3**
Bat & Ball Ent. Cen. TN14: S'oaks 6J **3**

Bat & Ball Rd. TN14: S'oaks 6J **3**
Bat & Ball Station (Rail) 6J **3**
Batchelors TN2: Pem 1J **35**
Bates Hill TN15: Igh 7A **6**
Battlefields Rd. TN15: Wro 1D **6**
Bayhall Rd. TN2: Tun W 3E **40** (6A 34)
Bayham Rd. TN2: Tun W 2J **37**
TN3: Bell G 5E **38**
TN13: S'oaks 1J **9**
BAYLEY'S HILL 1F **15**
Bayley's Hill TN14: S'oaks, Weald 2E **14**
Bayleys Hill Rd. TN8: Bou B 7E **14**
Beaconfields TN13: S'oaks 4F **9**
Beacon Ri. TN13: S'oaks 4G **9**
Beagles Wood Rd. TN2: Pem 2J **35**
(not continuous)
Beatrice Wilson Flats TN13: S'oaks 3H **9**
Beaulieu Rd. TN10: Tonb 3K **21**
Becket Ct. TN9: Tonb 7K **21**
(off Alexandra Rd.)
Beckets Fld. TN11: Pens 3A **26**
Beckets Pl. TN14: Otf 1J **3**
Bedford Rd. TN4: S'bgh 7J **27**
Bedford Ter. TN1: Tun W 5B **40** (7J 33)
Beecham Rd. TN10: Tonb 1C **22**
Beech Cl. TN2: Tun W 1A **38**
Beech Ct. TN2: Tun W 5B **34**
(Dell Dr.)
TN2: Tun W 7A **40**
(Montacute Rd.)
Beeches, The TN2: Tun W 4B **34**
Beech Hurst TN2: Pem 2H **35**
Beechin Wood La. TN15: Platt 7G **7**
Beechmont Cotts. TN13: Weald 1H **15**
Beechmont Ri. TN10: Tonb 1K **21**
Beechmont Rd. TN13: S'oaks 7H **9**
Beech Rd. TN13: S'oaks 3H **9**
Beech St. TN1: Tun W 1D **40** (5K 33)
Beechwood M. TN2: Tun W 5C **34**
Beechy Lees Rd. TN14: Otf 2K **3**
Belfield Rd. TN2: Pem 3H **35**
Belgrave Rd.
TN1: Tun W 1C **40** (5K 33)
Belgrove TN1: Tun W 5B **40** (7J 33)
Bell Cotts. TN11: Gold G 2K **23**
Bellows La. TN15: Bor G 5C **6**
Bells Farm Rd. TN11: E Peck 1C **24**
BELL'S YEW GREEN 5D **38**
Bells Yew Grn. Rd.
TN3: Bell G, Frant 6A **38**
BELTRING 3H **25**
Beltring Rd. TN4: Tun W 3J **33**
TN12: Pad W 3H **25**
Beltring Station (Rail) 3H **25**
Benhall Mill Rd. TN2: Tun W 2A **38**
TN3: Tun W 2C **38**
Bentham Hill TN3: S'bgh 7F **27**
Bentley's Mdw. TN15: Seal 5B **4**
Berkeley Cl. TN2: Pem 3H **35**
Berkeley Pl. TN1: Tun W 5B **40** (7J 33)
Berkeley Rd. TN1: Tun W 5B **40** (7J 33)
Berwick Way TN14: S'oaks 5H **3**
BESSELS GREEN 2D **8**
Bessels Grn. Rd. TN13: Bess G 1D **8**
Bessels Mdw. TN13: Bess G 2D **8**
Bessels Way TN13: Bess G 2D **8**
Betenson Av. TN13: S'oaks 7F **3**
Bethel Rd. TN13: S'oaks 1J **9**
Beulah Rd. TN1: Tun W 1D **40** (4K 33)
Beverley Cres. TN10: Tonb 1H **27**
Bewley La. TN15: Bor G, Plax 3A **12**
Bickley Rd. TN9: Tonb 7K **21**
Bickmore Way TN9: Tonb 4A **22**
BIDBOROUGH 4E **26**
Bidborough Ct. TN3: Bidb 5D **26**
Bidborough Ridge TN3: Bidb 4E **26**
TN4: Bidb 4E **26**
Bines, The TN12: Pad W 3G **31**
Birch Cl. TN2: Tun W 2B **34**
TN11: Hild 3F **21**

Birch Cl. TN12: Mat 7D **30**
TN13: S'oaks 1H **9**
Birches, The TN9: Tonb 1K **27**
Birchetts Av. TN3: Lang G 6A **32**
Birch Pl. TN13: S'oaks 2G **9**
Birch Rd. TN12: Pad W 2G **31**
Birch Way TN2: Tun W 2B **34**
Birchwood Av. TN4: S'bgh 5G **27**
Birchwood La. TN14: Dun G 1A **2**
Birdcage Wlk. TN1: Tun W ..5C **40** (6K **33**)
Bird in Hand St. TN3: Groom 4B **36**
Birkdale TN1: Tun W 3K **33**
Birken Rd. TN2: Tun W 3B **34**
Birling Dr. TN2: Tun W 1J **37**
Birling Pk. Av. TN2: Tun W 2K **37**
Birling Rd. TN2: Tun W 2J **37**
Bishop's Ct. TN4: Tun W 6G **33**
Bishop's Down TN4: Tun W 6G **33**
Bishop's Down Pk. Rd.
TN4: Tun W 5G **33**
Bishop's Down Rd. TN4: Tun W ...5G **33**
Bishops M. TN9: Tonb 7A **22**
Bishops Oak Ride TN10: Tonb 7K **17**
BITCHET GREEN 4F **11**
Blackberry Way TN12: Pad W 2G **31**
Blackhall La. TN15: S'oaks, God G ...1K **9**
Black Horse M. TN15: Bor G 5E **6**
Blackhorse M. TN2: Pem 3G **35**
BLACKHURST 4C **34**
Blackhurst La. TN2: Pem, Lang W ...4C **34**
(not continuous)
Blackhurst Lane Sports Cen. 3D **34**
Blackman's La. TN11: Hdlw 7H **19**
Blackmead TN13: Riv 6E **2**
Blacksole Cotts. TN15: Wro 1D **6**
Blacksole La. TN15: Wro 1D **6**
Blacksole Rd. TN15: Wro 1D **6**
Black's Yd. TN13: S'oaks 3J **9**
(off Bank St.)
Blackthorn Av. TN4: S'bgh 7A **28**
Blair Dr. TN13: S'oaks 1H **9**
BLAKES GREEN 3F **11**
Blakeway TN2: Tun W 2B **34**
Blatchington Rd.
TN2: Tun W 7B **40** (1J **37**)
Bligh's Ct. TN13: S'oaks 3J **9**
(off Bligh's Rd.)
Bligh's Mdw. TN13: S'oaks 3J **9**
(off High St.)
Bligh's Rd. TN13: S'oaks 3J **9**
Bligh's Wlk. TN13: S'oaks 3H **9**
(off Bligh's Rd.)
Blind La. TN12: Brenc 7H **31**
Bliss Way TN10: Tonb 2C **22**
Bluebell Walks TN12: Pad W 2G **31**
Bogey La. TN4: Tun W 5H **33**
Boleyn Rd. TN15: Kems'g 2A **4**
Bondfield Cl. TN4: S'bgh 7J **27**
Boneashe La. TN15: Platt 6H **7**
Bordyke TN9: Tonb 5A **22**
BOROUGH GREEN 5D **6**
Borough Green & Wrotham Station (Rail)
..........................5D **6**
Borough Grn. Rd. TN15: Bor G, Igh ..6B **6**
TN15: Wro 2E **6**
Bosville Av. TN13: S'oaks 1G **9**
Bosville Dr. TN13: S'oaks 1G **9**
Bosville Rd. TN13: S'oaks 1G **9**
Botany TN9: Tonb 6A **22**
Bottle Cotts. TN13: S'oaks 7G **3**
Bough Beech Nature Reserve 7A **14**
Bough Beech Reservoir Vis. Cen. ...7A **14**
Boundary, The TN3: Lang G 6D **32**
Boundary Rd. TN2: Tun W 1B **38**
Bounds Oak Way TN4: S'bgh 5G **27**
Bourchier Cl. TN13: S'oaks 4H **9**
Bourne Cl. TN9: Tonb 4B **22**
Bourne Ent. Cen. TN15: Bor G 4E **6**
Bourne La. TN9: Tonb 4B **22**
TN15: Plax 4D **12**

Bourne Pk. TN11: Gold G 2K **23**
Bourne Pl. TN11: Hild 7C **16**
Bourne Pl. Mdws. TN11: Hild 7C **16**
Bourne Va. TN15: Plax 5E **12**
Bowden Ct. TN15: Kems'g 2B **4**
Bowen Rd. TN4: R'hall 4D **32**
Bowlplex
Tunbridge Wells 1D **34**
Bowls Pl. TN12: Pad W 1G **31**
BOWZELL GREEN 4F **15**
Bowzell Rd. TN14: Weald 4F **15**
Bowzells La. TN14: Weald 6E **14**
Boyle Way TN12: E Peck 2H **25**
Boyne Pk. TN4: Tun W 2A **40** (5H **33**)
Bracken Cl. TN2: Tun W 4C **34**
Bracken Rd. TN2: Tun W 4C **34**
Brackens, The TN13: S'oaks 1J **9**
Bracken Wlk. TN10: Tonb 1K **21**
Bradbourne Ct. TN13: S'oaks 7H **3**
Bradbourne Pk. Rd. TN13: S'oaks ...1G **9**
Bradbourne Rd. TN13: S'oaks 7H **3**
Bradbourne Va. Rd. TN13: S'oaks ...7F **3**
Bradford St. TN9: Tonb 6K **21**
Bradley St. TN9: Tonb 5K **21**
Braeside Av. TN13: S'oaks 2F **9**
Braeside Cl. TN13: S'oaks 1F **9**
Bramble Cl. TN11: Hild 3G **21**
Bramble La. TN13: S'oaks 6H **9**
Bramble Wlk. TN2: Tun W 2B **34**
Bramley Gdns. TN12: Pad W 1E **30**
Bramley Rd. TN12: E Peck 1F **25**
Brampton Bank TN11: Tude 2J **29**
BRANBRIDGES 2G **25**
Branbridges Ind. Est. TN12: E Peck ..2G **25**
Branbridges Rd. TN12: E Peck ...1G **25**
Brantingham Cl. TN9: Tonb 1H **27**
Brattle Wood TN13: S'oaks 7H **9**
Breach Ho. TN15: Plax 6B **22**
Breedon Av. TN4: S'bgh 7H **27**
BRENCHLEY 7H **31**
Brenchley Rd. TN3: Brenc, Mat ...7G **31**
Brenchley Woods Nature Reserve ...7B **30**
Brendon Cl. TN2: Tun W 4B **34**
Brent, The TN10: Tonb 1A **22**
Bretland Rd. TN4: R'hall 5F **33**
Brewery La. TN13: S'oaks 3H **9**
Brian Cres. TN4: S'bgh 1K **33**
Briar Wlk. TN10: Tonb 1A **22**
Brickfields TN2: Pem 1J **35**
Brickmakers Mdws. TN15: Platt ..5G **7**
Brickworks Cl. TN9: Tonb 2J **27**
Brickworks Cotts. TN14: S'oaks ..5K **3**
Bridge Bus. Pk. TN12: Five G 1C **30**
Bridge Cl. TN9: Tonb 7A **22**
Bridge Ct. TN1: Tun W 4K **33**
Bridge Ho. TN4: Tun W 5A **22**
TN9: Tonb 5A **22**
(off High St.)
Bright Ridge TN4: S'bgh 1G **33**
Brindles Fld. TN9: Tonb 1J **27**
Brionne Gdns. TN9: Tonb 7B **22**
Brittains La. TN13: S'oaks 2F **9**
Britten Cl. TN10: Tonb 1D **22**
Broadcroft TN2: Tun W 2H **37**
Broad Gro. TN2: Tun W 1J **37**
Broadhoath TN15: Ivy H 4G **11**
Broadmead TN2: Tun W 2G **37**
Broadmead Av. TN2: Tun W 2H **37**
Broad Oak TN3: Groom 6C **36**
TN12: Brenc 7J **31**
Broad Oak Cl. TN2: Tun W 1H **37**
TN12: Brenc 7J **31**
Broadview Gdns. 6H **19**
Broad Wlk. TN15: S'oaks 6A **10**
Broadwater Ct. TN2: Tun W 2G **37**
BROADWATER DOWN 1H **37**
Broadwater Down TN2: Tun W ...2G **37**
Broadwater Forest 3C **36**
Broadwater Forest La.
TN3: Groom, Tun W 3B **36**

Broadwater La. TN2: Tun W 1H **37**
Broadwater Ri. TN2: Tun W ...7A **40** (1H **37**)
Broadwater Warren RSPB Nature Reserve
..........................4D **36**
Broadway, The TN11: Hdlw 6J **19**
(off High St.)
Brockway TN15: Bor G 5E **6**
Brockfield TN12: Five G 1B **30**
Brookdene TN12: Five G 1B **30**
Brookfield TN15: Kems'g 2A **4**
Brookfield Ct. TN4: S'bgh 7J **27**
Brookfields TN3: Hdlw 6J **19**
Brookhurst Gdns. TN4: S'bgh 5G **27**
Brooklands TN2: Tun W 2B **34**
Brook La. TN9: Tonb 5B **22**
TN15: Plax 5E **12**
Brookmead TN11: Hild 2G **21**
Brook Rd. TN12: Pad W 2A **34**
Brooks Cl. TN10: Tonb 7B **18**
Brookside Cotts. TN2: Tun W 4D **34**
BROOK STREET 1H **27**
Brook St. TN9: Tonb 7H **21**
Broomfield TN3: Bell G 5D **38**
Broomfield Rd. TN13: S'oaks 7F **3**
BROOMHILL BANK 3E **32**
Broomhill Pk. Rd. TN4: S'bgh 1G **33**
Broomhill Rd. TN3: R'hall, S'bgh ..3E **32**
Broom La. TN3: Lang G, Tun W ...7A **32**
Broom Pk. TN3: Lang G 6A **32**
Broughton Rd. TN14: Otf 1G **3**
Brunger's Wlk. TN10: Tonb 2K **21**
Brunswick Ter. TN1: Tun W ..6B **40** (7J **33**)
Bubblestone Rd. TN14: Otf 1H **3**
Buckhurst Av. TN13: S'oaks 3J **9**
Buckhurst La. TN13: S'oaks 3J **9**
Buckingham Rd.
TN1: Tun W 5C **40** (7K **33**)
Bucklers Cl. TN2: Tun W 6A **34**
Buckwell Pl. TN13: S'oaks 7J **9**
BUDD'S GREEN 1H **17**
BULLEN 1E **24**
Bullen La. TN12: E Peck 1E **24**
Bullfinch Cl. TN12: Pad W 3G **31**
TN13: Riv 7D **2**
Bullfinch Dene TN13: Riv 7D **2**
Bullfinch La. TN13: Riv 7D **2**
Bullingstone La. TN3: Speld 2A **32**
Bullion Cl. TN12: Pad W 2F **31**
Bull La. TN15: Wro 1E **6**
Bulls Pl. TN2: Pem 3H **35**
Bungalows, The TN11: Leigh 6A **20**
Bunny La. TN3: Tun W 4F **37**
Burdett Rd. TN4: R'hall 5D **32**
Burgess Rd. TN2: Tun W 3B **34**
Burton Ct. TN12: Pad W 2G **31**
Burwood Pk. TN2: Tun W 4C **34**
Bush Rd. TN12: E Peck 1E **24**
Bushy Gill TN3: Lang G 6C **32**
Busty La. TN15: Igh 6B **6**
Buttercup Cl. TN12: Pad W 3G **31**
Butts, The TN14: Otf 1H **3**
Byng Rd. TN4: Tun W 4G **33**
Byrneside TN11: Hild 3G **21**

Cabbage Stalk La. TN4: Tun W ...7G **33**
Cade La. TN13: S'oaks 6J **9**
Cadogan Gdns. TN1: Tun W ..2C **40** (5K **33**)
CAGE GREEN 2A **22**
Cage Grn. Rd. TN10: Tonb 2A **22**

Caistor Rd.—Cold Arbor Rd.

Caistor Rd. TN9: Tonb 6J 21
Caley Rd. TN2: Tun W 1B 34
Calverley Ct. TN1: Tun W 3E 40 (6A 34)
Calverley Hgts. *TN2: Tun W 5B 34*
(off Sandrock Rd.)
Calverley Pk. TN1: Tun W 3C 40 (6K 33)
Calverley Pk. Cres.
TN1: Tun W 3C 40 (6K 33)
Calverley Pk. Gdns.
TN1: Tun W 2D 40 (5K 33)
Calverley Rd. TN1: Tun W 2C 40 (5K 33)
Calverley Row TN1: Tun W 2C 40 (5K 33)
Calverley St. TN1: Tun W 2C 40 (5K 33)
Cambrian Rd. TN4: Tun W 2A 34
Cambridge Gdns.
TN2: Tun W 5D 40 (7K 33)
Cambridge Ho.
TN2: Tun W 5D 40 (7K 33)
Cambridge St. TN2: Tun W 4E 40 (6A 34)
Cambridge Vs. TN1: Tun W 2A 40
Camden Av. TN2: Pem 3G 35
Camden Ct. TN1: Tun W 1D 40 (5K 33)
TN2: Pem 3H 35
Camden Hill TN2: Tun W 4D 40 (6K 33)
CAMDEN PARK 7A 34
Camden Pk.
TN2: Tun W 5E 40 & 6E 40 (7A 34)
(not continuous)
Camden Rd. TN1: Tun W 2C 40 (5K 33)
TN13: S'oaks 7H 3
Camden Ter. TN15: Seal 6B 4
Campbell Rd. TN4: Tun W 3J 33
Cannon Bri. Ind. Est. TN9: Tonb 5B 22
Cannon La. TN9: Tonb 5B 22
Cannon Pk. TN12: Pad W 7G 25
Cannons Wharf TN9: Tonb 6A 22
Canterbury Cres. TN10: Tonb 2B 22
Canterbury Rd. TN2: Pem 3J 35
CAPEL 2K 29
Cardinal Cl. TN9: Tonb 7B 22
Carey's Fld. TN13: Dun G 5E 2
Carlton Cl. TN10: Tonb 7B 18
Carlton Cres. TN1: Tun W 2E 40 (5A 34)
Carlton Pde. TN13: S'oaks 7J 3
Carlton Rd. TN1: Tun W 2E 40 (5A 34)
Carpenters La. TN11: Hdlw 3G 19
Carrick Dr. TN13: S'oaks 1H 9
Carroty Wood Activity Cen. 6C 18
Carrs Cnr. TN1: Tun W 2D 40 (5K 33)
CARTER'S HILL 6D 10
Carter's Hill TN15: Under 1D 16
Carville Av. TN4: S'bgh 7H 27
Castle Ct. TN9: Tonb 4A 22
Castle Dr. TN15: Kems'g 2A 4
Castlefields TN9: Tonb 5K 21
CASTLE HILL 7K 31
Castle Rd. TN4: Tun W 3A 40 (7J 33)
Castle St. TN1: Tun W 5B 40 (7J 33)
TN4: S'bgh 6H 27
TN9: Tonb 5K 21
Castle Ter. TN11: Hdlw 6J 19
Castle Vw. TN11: Hdlw 6J 19
Catherine Pl. TN1: Tun W 2C 40 (5K 33)
Catts Pl. TN12: Pad W 4J 31
Cavalry Cl. TN10: Tonb 7C 18
Cavendish Av. TN13: S'oaks 7G 3
Cavendish Cl. TN10: Tonb 7B 18
Cavendish Ct. TN9: Tonb 5A 22
Cavendish Dr. TN2: Tun W 6D 40 (7K 33)
Caxton La. TN11: Hdlw 6J 19
Caysers Cft. TN12: E Peck 1E 24
Cecil Burns Lodge TN2: Tun W 7B 34
Cecil Kidby Ho. TN2: Tun W 3D 34
Cedar Ct. TN4: Tun W 4J 33
Cedar Cres. TN10: Tonb 7A 18
Cedar Lodge TN4: Tun W 6H 33
Cedar Ridge TN2: Tun W 3B 34
Cedars, The TN12: Pad W 1G 31
Cedar Ter. Rd. TN13: S'oaks 1J 9
Cemetery La. TN11: Hdlw 5K 19 & 6K 19
Centenary Cl. TN13: Dun G 5E 2
Chaffinch Way TN12: Pad W 3G 31
Chalket La. TN2: Pem 4G 35
Chalklin Bus. Pk. TN2: Tun W 7C 28
Challenger Cl. TN12: Pad W 2F 31
Chalybeate Spring 5A 40
(off The Pantiles)
Chancellor Ho. TN4: Tun W 6H 33
Chancellor Way TN13: S'oaks 7G 3
Chandos Rd. TN1: Tun W 4A 34
Chantlers Hill TN12: Pad W 5F 31
Chapel Pl. TN1: Tun W 5A 40 (7J 33)
Chapel Row TN15: Igh 6A 6
Chapel Vw. TN15: Igh 6A 6
Chapel Wlk. TN14: Ide H 1B 14
Chapman Way TN2: Tun W 1A 34
Charles Ct. TN2: Tun W 5A 34
Charles St. TN4: S'bgh 1J 33
Charlotte Cotts. TN11: Leigh 5B 20
Charlton's Way TN4: Tun W 1G 37
Charlton Ter. TN9: Tonb 5A 22
Charne, The TN14: Otf 2G 3
Charterhouse Dr. TN13: S'oaks 1G 9
Chart Vw. TN15: Kems'g 2D 4
Chartway TN13: S'oaks 2J 9
Chartwell Lodge TN4: Tun W 6H 33
Chase, The TN2: Tun W 5D 40 (7K 33)
TN10: Tonb 2A 22
TN15: Kems'g 1A 4
Chatham Hill Rd. TN14: S'oaks 6J 3
Chaucer Bus. Pk. TN15: Kems'g 3F 5
Chaucer Gdns. TN9: Tonb 1H 27
Chenies Cl. TN2: Tun W 2J 37
Cherry Gdns. Hill TN3: Groom 7A 36
Cherry Gro. TN10: Tonb 2C 22
Cherry Orchard, The TN11: Hdlw 5J 19
Cherry Tree Rd. TN2: Tun W 1G 37
TN10: Tonb 7B 18
Cherwell Cl. TN10: Tonb 2K 21
Chesfield Cl. TN11: Hdlw 6K 19
Chester Av. TN2: Tun W 7B 34
Chesterfield Dr. TN13: Riv 6D 2
Chestnut Av. TN4: S'bgh 1J 33
Chestnut Cl. TN4: S'bgh 1K 33
Chestnut La. TN12: Mat 7D 30
TN13: S'oaks 2H 9
Chestnuts Cl. TN11: Tonb 7B 18
Chestnut Wlk. TN9: Tonb 5H 21
TN15: S'oaks 7A 10
CHEVENING 4A 2
Chevening Cross TN14: Chev 5A 2
Chevening Rd. TN13: Chip 4A 2
TN14: Chev 4A 2
Cheviot Cl. TN9: Tonb 3A 22
Chichester Dr. TN13: S'oaks 3F 9
Chichester Rd. TN9: Tonb 7J 21
CHIDLEY CROSS 1E 24
Chidley Cross Rd. TN12: E Peck 1E 24
Chieveley Dr. TN2: Tun W 1B 38
Childsbridge Farm Pl. TN15: Seal 4A 4
Childsbridge La. TN15: Kems'g, Seal 2B 4
Childsbridge Way TN15: Seal 5B 4
Childs Way TN15: Wro 1D 6
Chilston Cl. TN4: Tun W 4J 33
Chilston Rd. TN4: Tun W 4J 33
Chiltern Wlk. TN2: Tun W 5B 34
Chiltern Way TN9: Tonb 3A 22
CHIPSTEAD 7C 2
Chipstead La. TN13: Chip, Riv 7C 2
Chipstead Pk. TN13: Chip 7D 2
Chipstead Pk. Cl. TN13: Chip 7C 2
Chipstead Pl. Gdns. TN13: Chip 7C 2
Chipstead Sailing Club 7C 2
Chipstead Sq. TN13: Chip 7C 2
Christ Chu. Av.
TN1: Tun W 4B 40 (6J 33)
Church Fld. TN13: Riv 7F 3
Church Fld. Cotts. TN15: Seal 5B 4
Church Hill TN11: Leigh 5B 20
TN15: Plax 5C 12
Church La. TN3: Frant 6K 37
TN9: Tonb 5A 22
TN12: Cap 3K 29
TN12: E Peck 1F 25
TN15: Kems'g 2D 4
Church Rd. TN1: Tun W 3A 40 (6H 33)
TN2: Pem 7H 29
TN4: S'bgh 6H 27
TN4: Tun W 3A 40 (6H 33)
TN11: Hild 1F 21
TN12: Pad W 1G 31
TN14: Weald 3H 15
TN15: Ivy H, Seal 1G 11
TN15: Seal 6B 4
Church St. TN9: Tonb 5A 22
TN11: Hdlw 6J 19
TN15: Seal 6C 4
Church Vs. TN13: Riv 7E 2
Cinderhill Wood Caravan Site
TN12: Mat 7C 30
Civic Way TN1: Tun W 2B 40
Clanricarde Gdns.
TN1: Tun W 3B 40 (6J 33)
Clanricarde Rd.
TN1: Tun W 3B 40 (6J 33)
Clare Av. TN9: Tonb 6H 21
Claremont Ct. *TN4: Tun W 2A 34*
(off Nth. Farm Rd.)
Claremont Gdns.
TN2: Tun W 5D 40 (7K 33)
Claremont Rd. TN1: Tun W 5C 40 (7K 33)
Clarence Lodge TN1: Tun W 4A 40
Clarence Rd. TN1: Tun W 3B 40 (6J 33)
Clarence Row TN1: Tun W 3B 40 (6J 33)
Clarendon Gdns.
TN2: Tun W 7A 40 (1J 37)
Clarendon Pl. TN13: S'oaks 3G 9
Clarendon Rd. TN13: S'oaks 2G 9
Clarendon Way TN2: Tun W 7A 40 (1H 37)
Clare Way TN13: S'oaks 6J 9
Clavadel Rd. TN12: Pad W 1G 31
(not continuous)
CLAYGATE 2D 18
CLAYGATE CROSS 2E 12
Claygate Cross TN11: S'brne 2D 18
Claygate La. TN11: S'brne 1D 18
Claygate Rd. ME18: Ladd 3K 25
Clearway ME19: Addtn 3K 7
Cleavesland ME18: Ladd 2K 25
Cleeve Av. TN2: Tun W 7B 34
Clenches Farm TN13: S'oaks 5G 9
Clenches Farm La. TN13: S'oaks 4G 9
Clenches Farm Rd. TN13: S'oaks 4G 9
Cleveland TN2: Tun W 5B 34
Cleves Rd. TN15: Kems'g 2A 4
Clifton Cotts. TN2: Tun W 1B 34
Clifton Pl. TN1: Tun W 5C 40 (7K 33)
Clifton Rd. TN2: Tun W 2A 34
Clockhouse TN2: Tun W 3D 34
Clock Ho. La. TN13: S'oaks 1G 9
Close, The TN3: Groom 6C 36
TN4: Tun W 1A 34
TN13: S'oaks 2E 8
TN15: Bor G 4E 6
TN15: Igh 6B 6
Clover Way TN12: Pad W 3G 31
Club Cotts. TN11: Hild 6F 17
Clyde Rd. TN10: Tonb 1A 22
Coach & Horses Pas.
TN2: Tun W 6A 40
Coach Rd. TN4: R'hall 5E 32
TN15: Igh, Ivy H 2J 11
Cobbett's Ride TN2: Tun W 1H 37
Cobbs Cl. TN12: Pad W 2F 31
Cobden Rd. TN13: S'oaks 1J 9
Cobhams TN3: Speld 1C 32
Cobs Cl. TN15: Igh 6A 6
Cogate Rd. TN12: Pad W 2E 30
Colbran Way TN4: Lang G, R'hall 6D 32
Cold Arbor Rd. TN13: Bess G 2D 8

44 A-Z Tunbridge Wells, Sevenoaks & Tonbridge

D

Dukes Rd. TN1: Tun W	.1E **40** (4A **34**)
Dunckley Vs. ME19: Addtn	.3K 7
Dundale Rd. TN3: Mat, Tun W	.2E **38**
TN12: Mat	.1J **39**
DUNK'S GREEN	.7E 12
Dunk's Grn. Rd. TN11: S'brne	.1E 18
Dunorlan Farm Cotts.	
TN2: Tun W	.5C **34**
Dunorlan Pk.	.6B **34**
Dunstan Gro. TN4: Tun W	.3K **33**
Dunstan Rd. TN4: Tun W	.3K **33**
DUNTON GREEN	.5E 2
Dunton Green Station (Rail)	.4E 2
Durlings Orchard TN15: Igh	.6B 6
Dux Hill TN15: Plax	.4D 12
Dux La. TN15: Plax	.4D 12
Dynes, The TN15: Kems'g	.2K 3
Dynes Rd. TN15: Kems'g	.2K 3
Dynevor Rd. TN4: Tun W	.2A **34**

E

Eaglestone Cl. TN15: Bor G	.4E 6
Eardley Rd. TN13: S'oaks	.2H 9
Earl's Rd. TN4: Tun W	.5H **33**
E. Cliff Rd. TN4: Tun W	.3J **33**
Eastfield Gdns. TN10: Tonb	.2C **22**
Eastlands Cl. TN4: Tun W	.2G **37**
Eastlands Rd. TN4: Tun W	.2G **37**
EAST PECKHAM	.1F 25
East St. TN9: Tonb	.5A **22**
Eastwell Cl. TN12: Five G	.2E **30**
Edenhurst TN13: S'oaks	.3G 9
Eden Rd. TN1: Tun W	.6B **40** (7J **33**)
Eden Wlk. TN1: Tun W	.6B **40** (7J **33**)
Edgar Rd. TN15: Kems'g	.2A 4
Edison Ct. TN4: Tun W	.4J **33**
Edward St. TN4: R'hall	.5D **32**
TN4: S'bgh	.7H **27**
Egdean Wlk. TN13: S'oaks	.1J 9
Eggpie La. TN11: Hild	.5J 15
TN14: Weald	.5J 15
Eldon Way TN12: Pad W	.1F **31**
Elgar Cl. TN10: Tonb	.1C **22**
Elizabeth Garlick Ct.	
TN1: Tun W	.1C **40**
Ellis Cl. TN12: Five G	.1B **30**
Elmfield Cl. TN14: Weald	.4H 15
Elm Gro. TN11: Hild	.3H **21**
Elmhurst Av. TN2: Pem	.1H **35**
Elm La. TN10: Tonb	.4A **22**
Elm Rd. TN4: S'bgh	.7H **27**
Elms, The TN4: R'hall	.6E **32**
Elmshurst Gdns. TN10: Tonb	.7A 18
Elmstead Cl. TN13: Riv	.7E 2
Elphick's Pl. TN2: Tun W	.2K **37**
Ely Ct. TN1: Tun W	.2C **40** (5K **33**)
Ely Gdns. TN10: Tonb	.3B **22**
ELY GRANGE	.5A **38**
Ely La. TN1: Tun W	.2C **40** (5K **33**)
Emily Jackson Cl. TN13: S'oaks	.2H 9
Ensfield Rd. TN11: Leigh	.7A **20** & 2C **26**
Enterprise Ho. TN9: Tonb	.6K **21**
(off Avebury Av.)	
ERIDGE GREEN	.6D **36**
Eridge Pk. TN3: Eri G	.6E **36**
Eridge Rd. TN3: Eri G	.7D **36**
TN4: Tun W	.6A **40** (2G **37**)
Erskine Ho. TN13: S'oaks	.3G 9
Erskine Pk. Rd. TN4: R'hall	.5D **32**
Essex Cl. TN2: Tun W	.2H **37**
Estridge Way TN10: Tonb	.2D **22**
Etherington Hill	
TN3: S'bgh, Speld	.2D **32**
Evelyn Rd. TN14: Otf	.1J 3
Ewehurst La. TN3: Speld	.3B **32**
Ewins Cl. TN12: Pad W	.2G **31**
Exchange Ct. TN9: Tonb	.5A **22**
Exchange M. TN4: Tun W	.4J **33**

Exedown Rd. TN15: Wro	.1A 6
Exeter Cl. TN10: Tonb	.3A **22**

F

Fairfield Av. TN2: Tun W	.4A **34**
Fairfield Cl. TN15: Kems'g	.3C 4
Fairfield Cres. TN9: Tonb	.7A **22**
Fairfield Rd. TN15: Bor G	.4D 6
Fairfield Way TN11: Hild	.2G **21**
Fairlight Cl. TN4: S'bgh	.6J **27**
Fairlight Rd. TN10: Tonb	.3K **21**
Fairmile Rd. TN2: Tun W	.4C **34**
Fairview Cl. TN9: Tonb	.2K **27**
Fairview La. TN3: Tun W	.2D **36**
Fairways, The TN4: S'bgh	.1J **33**
Falmouth Pl. TN12: Five G	.1C **30**
Faraday Ride TN10: Tonb	.7B 18
Farmcombe Cl.	
TN2: Tun W	.6D **40** (7K **33**)
Farmcombe La.	
TN2: Tun W	.5C **40** (7K **33**)
Farmcombe Rd.	
TN2: Tun W	.5C **40** (7K **33**)
Farm Ct. TN4: Tun W	.2G **37**
Farmground Cl. TN9: Tonb	.7C **22**
Farm La. TN10: Tonb	.3J **21**
Farm Rd. TN14: S'oaks	.5J 3
Farnaby Dr. TN13: S'oaks	.4F 9
Farnham Beeches TN3: Lang G	.5C **32**
Farnham Cl. TN3: Lang G	.6C **32**
Farnham La. TN3: Lang G	.6C **32**
TN4: R'hall	.6C **32**
Farnham Pl. TN3: Lang G	.6C **32**
Farrance Ct. TN1: Tun W	.2D **40** (5K **33**)
Farthingfield TN15: Wro	.1E 6
FAWKE COMMON	.5C 10
Fawke Comn. TN15: Under, God G	.4C 10
Fawke Wood Rd. TN15: Under	.6C 10
Fell Mead TN12: E Peck	.1F 25
Fellowes Way TN11: Hild	.2G **21**
Fen Mdw. TN15: Igh	.3A 6
Fen Pond Cotts. TN15: Igh	.3A 6
Fen Pond Rd. TN15: Igh, Wro	.1A 6
Ferbies TN3: Speld	.2C **32**
Ferbies Cl. TN3: Speld	.2C **32**
Ferdinand Ter. TN3: Groom	.5C **36**
(off Corseley Rd.)	
Fern Cl. TN3: Frant	.7K **37**
FERNDALE	.4A **34**
Ferndale TN2: Tun W	.1E **40** (5A **34**)
TN13: S'oaks	.7J 3
Ferndale Cl. TN2: Tun W	.5A **34**
Ferndale Gdns. TN2: Tun W	.5A **34**
Ferndale Point TN2: Tun W	.5A **34**
Fernholt TN10: Tonb	.7A 18
Fernhurst Cres. TN4: S'bgh	.6J **27**
Ferns, The TN1: Tun W	.2E **40** (5A **34**)
TN15: Platt	.5G 7
Fernside La. TN13: S'oaks	.7K 9
Ferox Hall TN9: Tonb	.5A **22**
Ferringham TN4: Tun W	.1A **40** (5H **33**)
Fiennes Way TN13: S'oaks	.5J 9
FIG STREET	.6G 9
Fig St. TN14: S'oaks	.7F 9
Filmer La. TN14: S'oaks	.6A 4
Filston La. TN14: Otf	.1D 2
Firs Ct. TN4: Tun W	.3H **33**
First St. TN3: Lang G	.6B **32**
Fir Tree Cl. TN11: Hild	.2G **21**
Fir Tree Rd. TN4: Tun W	.6H **33**
Fishers Oak TN14: S'oaks	.7K 9
Five Furlongs TN12: Pad W	.1K **31**
FIVE OAK GREEN	.1B **30**
Five Oak Grn. Rd.	
TN11: Five G, Tonb, Tude	.1C **28**
TN11: Five G, Tude	.2H **29**
TN12: Five G	.2H **29**

FIVE WENTS	.7D **30**
Flaxmore Pk. TN4: S'bgh	.6J **27**
Fleming Way TN10: Tonb	.7C 18
FLETCHER'S GREEN	.5J 15
Fleur de Lis Cotts. TN11: Leigh	.6B **20**
Floats, The TN13: Riv	.6E 2
Florance La. TN3: Groom	.6B **36**
Flowerfield TN14: Otf	.2F 3
Floyd Cl. TN4: Tun W	.2J **33**
Foalhurst Cl. TN10: Tonb	.3C **22**
Foal Hurst Wood Nature Reserve	.3D **30**
Fordcombe Rd. TN11: Pens	.3A **26**
Ford La. ME19: Tros	.3K 7
TN15: Wro H	.3K 7
Ford Pl. Cotts. TN15: Wro H	.2J 7
Forest Gro. TN10: Tonb	.2A **22**
Forest Rd. TN2: Tun W	.7E **40** (2J **37**)
TN12: Pad W	.2F **31**
Forest Way TN2: Pem	.1H **35**
TN2: Tun W	.1A **38**
Forge, The TN12: Five G	.1B **30**
Forge Cl. TN11: Pens	.2B **26**
TN12: Five G	.1B **30**
Forge Cotts. TN14: Weald	.4J 15
Forge La. ME18: W Peck	.7K 13
Forge Rd. TN4: S'bgh	.7H **27**
Forge Sq. TN11: Leigh	.5B **20**
Forge Way TN12: Pad W	.1G **31**
Forstal, The TN2: Pem	.1H **35**
TN11: Hdlw	.6K 19
Forstall TN3: Lang G	.5C **32**
Forstall, The TN11: Leigh	.5C **20**
Fort Rd. TN14: Hals	.1C 2
Forum, The	
Tunbridge Wells	.5A **40** (7J **33**)
Fosse Bank Cl. TN9: Tonb	.1J **27**
Fosse Rd. TN9: Tonb	.5K **21**
Four Wents Cl. TN15: Bor G	.5D 6
Foxbury TN15: Platt	.5F 7
Foxbush TN11: Hild	.1E **20**
Foxgloves, The TN12: Pad W	.3H **31**
FOXHOLE	.7C **30**
Foxhole La. TN12: Mat	.7C **30**
Fox Lea TN15: Bor G	.5D 6
Framley Rd. TN10: Tonb	.1D **22**
Francis Rd. TN11: Hild	.1F **21**
Frankfield Ri. TN2: Tun W	.7A **40** (1J **37**)
Frank's Hollow Rd.	
TN3: Bidb, S'bgh	.7E **26**
Frank Woolley Rd. TN10: Tonb	.2D **22**
FRANT	.7K **37**
Frant Ct. TN3: Frant	.7K **37**
Frant Grn. Rd. TN3: Frant	.6K **37**
Frant Rd. TN2: Tun W	.6A **40** (7J **33**)
TN3: Frant, Tun W	.3J **37**
Frant Station (Rail)	.5D **38**
Freehold, The TN11: Hdlw	.5H 19
TN12: E Peck	.1F 25
Fremlin Cl. TN4: R'hall	.5D **32**
Friars Way TN2: Tun W	.3B **34**
Friezland Rd. TN4: S'oaks	.1F **37**
Frog La. TN1: Tun W	.5B **40** (7J **33**)
Frome Ct. TN10: Tonb	.2K **21**
Fuggles Cl. TN12: Pad W	.2E **30**
Fuller St. TN15: Seal	.5D 4
Furnival Ct. TN2: Tun W	.2H **37**
Furzefield Av. TN3: Speld	.1C **32**

G

Gainsborough Gdns. TN10: Tonb	.2C **22**
Gallards Almshouses TN4: S'bgh	.7J **27**
Garden Cotts. TN11: Leigh	.5C **20**
Garden Ct. TN13: S'oaks	.7K 3
(off Garden Rd.)	
Garden Ho. TN1: Tun W	.2D **40**
Garden Rd. TN1: Tun W	.1D **40** (5K **33**)
TN9: Tonb	.5A **22**
TN13: S'oaks	.7K 3

Helen Keller Cl. TN10: Tonb 2B 22
Hempson Ct. TN4: Tun W 4J 33
Hendal Hill TN3: Groom 6A 36
Henham Gdns. TN12: E Peck 1G 25
Henley Cl. TN2: Tun W 4A 34
Henley Rd. TN12: Pad W 1G 31
HENWOOD GREEN 3J 35
Henwood Grn. Rd. TN2: Pem 2H 35
Henwoods Cres. TN2: Pem 3H 35
Henwoods Mt. TN2: Pem 3J 35
Hermitage Ct. TN9: Tonb 5A 22
Hern, The TN15: Crouc 7G 7
Herons Way TN2: Pem 1J 35
Heskett Pk. TN2: Pem 2J 35
Higham Gdns. TN10: Tonb 2D 22
Higham La. TN3: Bell G 6F 39
    TN10: Tonb 3C 22
    TN11: Tonb 5C 18
Higham School Rd. TN10: Tonb 1C 22
HIGHAM WOOD 2C 22
High Beeches TN2: Tun W 3B 34
HIGH BROOMS 1A 34
High Brooms Rd. TN4: Tun W 1K 33
High Brooms Station (Rail) 2A 34
High Cross Rd. TN15: Ivy H 4K 11
Highfield Cl. TN2: Pem 3H 35
Highfield Rd. TN4: Tun W 2A 34
    TN15: Kems'g 1A 4
Highgrove TN2: Tun W 2J 37
High Hilden Cl. TN10: Tonb 3J 21
High Ho. La. TN11: Hdlw 6F 19
Highlands TN2: Tun W 2B 34
Highlands Pk. TN15: Seal 6A 4
High Rocks .1D 36
High Rocks Halt Station
    Spa Valley Railway 1D 36
High Rocks La. TN3: Tun W 1D 36
High St. TN1: Tun W 5B 40 (7J 33)
    TN2: Pem 3F 35
    TN3: Bidb 5E 26
    TN3: Frant 6A 38
    TN4: R'hall 5D 32
    TN9: Tonb 6K 21
    TN11: Hdlw 6J 19
    TN11: Leigh 6A 20
    TN11: Pens 2B 26
    TN12: Brenc 7H 31
    TN13: Chip 7C 2
    TN13: S'oaks 3J 9
    TN14: Otf .1G 3
    TN15: Bor G 5D 6
    TN15: Kems'g 2D 4
    TN15: Seal 6B 4
    TN15: Wro 1E 6
High Woods La. TN2: Tun W 7B 34
    TN3: Tun W 7E 34
Hilbert Cl. TN2: Tun W 4A 34
Hilbert Rd. TN2: Tun W 3A 34
Hilbert Woods Nature Reserve 3A 34
Hilden Av. TN11: Hild 3H 21
HILDENBOROUGH 2G 21
Hildenborough Rd. TN11: Leigh 5B 20
    TN11: S'brne, Under 2F 17
Hildenborough Station (Rail) 1D 20
Hildenbrook Farm TN11: Hild 4G 17
Hildenfields TN10: Tonb 3J 21
Hilden Golf Course 2D 20
Hilden Health & Fitness Club 2D 20
HILDEN PARK 2H 21
Hilden Pk. Rd. TN11: Hild 3H 21
Hillborough Av. TN13: S'oaks 7K 3
Hill Crest TN13: S'oaks 7G 3
Hillcrest TN4: S'bgh 1K 33
Hillcrest Dr. TN2: Tun W 2B 34
Hillfield Pl. TN13: Dun G 5D 2
Hillfield Rd. TN13: Dun G 5E 2
Hillgarth TN4: S'bgh 1J 33
Hillingdon Av. TN13: S'oaks 6J 3
Hillingdon Ri. TN13: S'oaks 7K 3
Hillside TN9: Tonb 1J 27

Hillside Rd. TN13: S'oaks 1K 9
    TN15: Kems'g 2B 4
Hill St. TN1: Tun W 1C 40 (4K 33)
Hillswood La. TN3: Tun W 3B 36
HILL TOP 7J 31
Hilltop TN9: Tonb 1K 27
Hill Vw. TN15: Bor G 5E 6
Hillview TN15: Bor G 1D 12
Hill Vw. Cl. TN15: Bor G 5E 6
Hill Vw. Rd. TN4: R'hall 5E 32
    TN11: Hild 2H 21
Hitchen Hatch La. TN13: S'oaks 2G 9
Hitchen Hatch Pl. TN13: S'oaks 1H 9
Hither Chantlers TN3: Lang G 7C 32
HOAD COMMON 2A 18
Holden Cnr. TN4: S'bgh 7G 27
Holden Pk. Rd. TN4: S'bgh 1H 33
Holden Rd. TN4: S'bgh 7G 27
Holder Ho. TN9: Tonb 6B 22
Holford St. TN9: Tonb 6K 21
Hollin Cl. TN4: Tun W 5H 33
Hollow Trees Dr. TN11: Leigh 5C 20
Holly Bank TN12: Brenc 7H 31
Hollybush Cl. TN13: S'oaks 2J 9
Hollybush Ct. TN13: S'oaks 2J 9
Holly Bush La. TN13: S'oaks 2J 9
Hollybush Sports Complex 1K 9
Hollyshaw Cl. TN2: Tun W . . .5E 40 (7A 34)
Holmesdale Rd. TN13: S'oaks 1J 9
Holmewood Ridge TN3: Lang G 6A 32
Holmewood Rd. TN4: Tun W 2A 34
Holmhurst Cl. TN4: Tun W 5H 33
Holyoake Ter. TN13: S'oaks 2G 9
Homedean Rd. TN13: Chip 7C 2
Home Farm Cl. TN11: Leigh 4C 20
Home Farm Ct. TN3: Frant 6A 38
Home Farm La. TN2: Tun W 1C 34
Homefield Rd. TN13: Riv 7E 2
Homestead, The TN3: Groom 5C 36
Homewood Rd. TN3: Lang G 6B 32
Homlesdale Bus. Cen. TN15: Platt 4G 7
Honey Pot La. TN15: Kems'g 4D 4
Hoopers Yd. TN13: S'oaks 4J 9
Hope Av. TN11: Hdlw 5H 19
Hop Farm Family Pk. 4G 25
Hopfield Cl. TN14: Otf 1J 3
Hopgarden La. TN13: S'oaks 6G 9
Hopgarden Rd. TN13: S'oaks 2B 22
Hop Pocket La. TN12: Pad W 1F 31
Hopwood Gdns. TN4: Tun W 3J 33
Hopwood Pl. TN4: Tun W 3J 33
                    (off Culverden Down)
Horizon Cl. TN4: S'bgh 1K 33
Hornbeam Av. TN4: S'bgh 7B 28
Hornbeam Cl. TN12: Pad W 3F 31
Horns Lodge TN11: Tonb 6A 18
Horns Lodge La. TN11: Hild, Tonb 6H 17
HOSPICE IN THE WEALD 7H 29
Hospital Rd. TN13: S'oaks 6J 3
Houselands Rd. TN9: Tonb 5K 21
Howard Dr. TN10: Tonb 2B 22
Howard Gdns. TN2: Tun W 7A 40 (1J 37)
Howlands TN15: Wro 1D 6
Howlands Ct. TN15: Wro 1D 6
                    (off Howlands)
Hubbard's Hill TN13: Weald 1H 15
    TN14: Weald 2H 15
Humboldt Ct. TN1: Tun W 4B 34
HUNGERSHALL PARK 7G 33
Hungershall Pk. TN4: Tun W 7F 33
Hungershall Pk. Cl. TN4: Tun W 7F 33
Hunsdon Dr. TN13: S'oaks 1H 9
Hunter Seal TN11: Leigh 5G 21
Hunters Way TN2: Tun W 1B 34
Huntley Gdns. TN4: Tun W 3G 33
Huntleys Pk. TN4: Tun W 4H 33
Hunt Rd. TN10: Tonb 1C 22
Hunts Farm Cl. TN15: Bor G 5E 6
Huntsman La. TN15: Wro H 3J 7
Hurlingham Cl. TN10: Tonb 7B 18

Hurst, The TN2: Tun W 2C 34
    TN11: Rough 5H 13
    TN15: Crouc 3G 13
Hurst Farm Rd. TN14: Weald 3H 15
Hurst La. TN14: Weald 4H 15
Hurst Way TN13: S'oaks 5J 9
Hurstwood La. TN4: Tun W 5G 33
Hurstwood Pk. TN4: Tun W 6H 33
Hyders Forge TN15: Plax 5E 12
                    (not continuous)
Hythe Cl. TN4: S'bgh 7J 27

I

Ide Hill Rd. TN8: Bou B 7A 14
    TN14: Ide H . . . . .4A 14 & 2A 14
IGHTHAM 6A 6
Ightham By-Pass TN15: Igh 6A 6
IGHTHAM COMMON 1K 11
Ightham Mote 5J 11
Ightham Rd. TN11: S'brne 7A 12
    TN15: S'brne 7A 12
Impala Gdns. TN4: Tun W 3K 33
Ingleborough La. TN15: Platt 4H 7
Inner London Rd.
    TN1: Tun W 3A 40 (6J 33)
Invicta Bus. Pk. TN15: Wro 2G 7
Ironstones TN3: Lang G 6D 32
Irving Ho. TN1: Tun W 1D 40 (4K 33)
Ismays Rd. TN15: Igh, Ivy H 3K 11
Ives Rd. TN9: Tonb 6H 21
IVY HATCH 4K 11
Ivy Ho. La. TN13: Dun G 3D 2
    TN14: Otf .3D 2
Ivy La. TN3: Bell G 5E 38

J

Jackwood Ct. TN1: Tun W 4K 33
Jackwood Way TN1: Tun W . . .1C 40 (4K 33)
James Cl. TN11: Hdlw 5K 19
Jeffery Harrison Vis. Cen. 6F 3
Johnsons Cl. TN15: Seal 6B 4
John Spare Ct. TN4: Tun W 3J 33
                    (off Whitefield Rd.)
John St. TN4: Tun W 4J 33
Jubilee Cotts. TN14: S'oaks 5H 3
Jubilee Cres. TN15: Igh 6A 6
Jubilee Ri. TN15: Seal 6B 4
Judd Rd. TN9: Tonb 1K 27
Julians Cl. TN13: S'oaks 5G 9
Julians Way TN13: S'oaks 5G 9
Juniper Cl. TN4: S'bgh 7B 28

K

Keel Gdns. TN4: S'bgh 1G 33
Kelchers La. TN11: Gold G 2K 23
Kelsey Ho. TN4: Tun W 4J 33
Kelvin Cl. TN10: Tonb 7B 18
Kemble Cl. TN2: Tun W 2C 34
KEMSING 2D 4
Kemsing Down Nature Reserve 1B 4
Kemsing Heritage Cen. 2D 4
Kemsing Rd. TN15: Kems'g, Wro 1H 5
Kemsing Station (Rail) 4F 5
Kendal Cl. TN9: Tonb 4A 22
Kendal Dr. TN9: Tonb 5A 22
Kendal Pk. TN4: Tun W 4G 33
Kennedy Gdns. TN13: S'oaks 1J 9
Kennet Rd. TN10: Tonb 2A 22
Kent & Sussex Crematorium
    TN2: Tun W 2K 37
Kent Cl. TN12: Pad W 2G 31
Kentish Gdns. TN2: Tun W 2G 37
Kentish Mans. TN1: Tun W 5A 40
Kent Rd. TN4: Tun W 3J 33

Pembury Rd. TN2: Tun W 3E 40 (6A 34)
TN9: Tonb 7K 21
TN11: Tonb, Tude, Tun W 2B 28
Pembury Walks TN2: Pem 6E 28
TN11: Tonb 6E 28
Pendennis Rd. TN13: S'oaks 1H 9
Penfolds Cl. TN10: Tonb 2A 22
Pennine Wlk. TN2: Tun W 4B 34
Pennington Mnr. TN4: S'bgh 6J 27
Pennington Pl. TN4: S'bgh 6K 27
Pennington Rd. TN4: S'bgh 6H 27
Penn's Yd. TN2: Pem 3G 35
Penruddocke Ho. TN10: Tonb 3A 22
PENSHURST 2B 26
Penshurst Place & Gardens 2B 26
Penshurst Rd. TN3: Bidb 5A 26
TN3: Speld 1A 32
TN11: Bidb, Pens 5A 26
TN11: Leigh, Pens . . . . .6A 20 & 1A 26
TN11: Pens 1A 32
Pen Way TN10: Tonb 2C 22
Petersfield TN2: Pem 1J 35
Petley Ct. Almshouses TN9: Tonb 7K 21
(off Pembury Rd.)
Philpots La. TN11: Hild, Leigh 2A 20
Pickmoss La. TN14: Otf 1G 3
Pierce Mill La. TN11: E Peck, Hdlw . . .2B 24
Pikefish La. TN12: Pad W 6K 25
Pilgrims Way TN13: Dun G 2C 2
(not continuous)
TN14: Otf .1K 3
TN15: Kems'g 1E 4
TN15: Wro 1D 6
(Battlefields Rd.)
TN15: Wro 1E 6
(Gravesend Rd.)
Pilgrims Way Cotts. TN15: Kems'g . . .2C 4
Pilgrims Way E. TN14: Otf 1J 3
Pilgrims Way W. TN14: Otf 2D 2
Pillar Box La. TN11: Hdlw 1H 19
TN15: Seal 7G 5
Pinehurst TN14: S'oaks 6A 4
Pineneedle La. TN13: S'oaks 1H 9
Pine Ridge TN10: Tonb 1K 21
Pines, The TN14: S'oaks 6K 3
Pine Tree La. TN15: Ivy H 3J 11
Pine Vw. TN15: Platt 5G 7
Pinewood Av. TN14: S'oaks 6K 3
Pinewood Cl. TN12: Pad W 2F 31
Pinewood Ct. TN4: S'bgh 7J 27
Pinewood Gdns. TN4: S'bgh 7J 27
Pinewood Rd. TN2: Tun W 4B 34
Pink All. TN2: Tun W 5A 40
Pinkham TN12: E Peck 2G 25
Pinkham Gdns. TN12: E Peck 1G 25
Pinnacle, The TN13: S'oaks 2G 9
Pinnacles Cl. TN10: Tonb 2A 22
Pippin Rd. TN12: E Peck 1F 25
Pippins Cl. TN10: Tonb 2A 22
PITTSWOOD 6E 18
Pittswood TN11: Hdlw 6F 19
Pittswood Cotts. TN11: Hdlw 6E 18
Pixot Hill TN12: Brenc 7H 31
Plane Wlk. TN10: Tonb 7A 18
Platt Comn. TN15: Platt 5G 7
Platt Ind. Est. TN15: Platt 4F 7
Platt Mill Cl. TN15: Platt 5F 7
Platt Mill Ter. TN15: Platt 5F 7
PLAXTOL 5C 12
Plaxtol La. TN15: Plax 5A 12
PLAXTOL SPOUTE 5E 12
Plough Hill TN15: Bor G 1D 12
Plummers Cft. TN13: Dun G 6E 2
Plymouth Dr. TN13: S'oaks 2J 9
Plymouth Pk. TN13: S'oaks 2J 9
Pocket Hill TN13: S'oaks 6G 9
Point Cnr. TN11: S'brne 1D 18
Polesden Rd. TN2: Tun W 7B 34
Polhill TN14: Hals 1C 2
Polley Cl. TN2: Pem 2H 35

Pond La. TN15: Ivy H 3G 11
Pontoise Cl. TN13: S'oaks 7F 3
Poona Rd. TN1: Tun W 5D 40 (7K 33)
Poppy Mdw. TN12: Pad W 3G 31
Portland Cl. TN10: Tonb 7B 18
Portman Pk. TN9: Tonb 4A 22
Postern Ind. Est. TN9: Tonb 6B 22
Postern La. TN11: Tonb 5B 22
Post Office Sq. TN1: Tun W . . .4B 40 (6J 33)
Potash La. TN15: Platt 6G 7
Poult Wood Golf Course 5D 18
Pound, The TN12: E Peck 1F 25
Pound Ho. TN11: Hdlw 6J 19
(off Maidstone Rd.)
Pound La. TN13: S'oaks 2J 9
Pound Rd. TN12: E Peck 1E 24
POUNDSBRIDGE 1A 32
Poundsbridge La. TN11: Pens 6A 26
Pounsley Rd. TN13: Dun G 6E 2
Powdermill Cl. TN4: S'bgh 1A 34
Powder Mill La.
TN4: S'bgh, Tun W 2J 33
TN11: Leigh 5C 20
(not continuous)
POWDER MILLS 5G 21
Prall's La. TN12: Mat 6E 30
Preston Rd. TN9: Tonb 6J 21
Priestley Dr. TN10: Tonb 7B 18
Primrose Wlk. TN12: Pad W 3G 31
Princes St. TN1: Tun W 4E 40 (6A 34)
Priory Gro. TN9: Tonb 7K 21
Priory Rd. TN9: Tonb 7K 21
Priory St. TN9: Tonb 7K 21
Priory Wlk. TN9: Tonb 7K 21
Progressive Ho. TN12: Pad W 7G 25
Prospect Pk. TN4: S'bgh 7H 27
Prospect Rd. TN2: Tun W 4D 40 (6K 33)
TN4: S'bgh 7H 27
TN13: S'oaks 1J 9
Providence Cotts. TN3: Groom 5C 36
(off Corseley Rd.)
Prudence Cotts. TN14: Weald 4H 15
Pudding La. TN15: Seal 6B 4
Pump Ter. TN1: Tun W 1D 40
Purcell Av. TN10: Tonb 1D 22
Pychers Pl. TN2: Pem 3H 35

Q

Quaker Cl. TN13: S'oaks 1K 9
Quakers Hall La. TN13: S'oaks 7J 3
Quantock Cl. TN2: Tun W 4B 34
Quarry Bank TN9: Tonb 1J 27
Quarry Cotts. TN13: S'oaks 1G 9
Quarry Gdns. TN9: Tonb 7J 21
Quarry Hill TN13: S'oaks 1K 9
Quarry Hill Pde. TN9: Tonb 7K 21
Quarry Hill Rd. TN9: Tonb 1J 27
TN15: Bor G 6D 6
Quarry Ri. TN9: Tonb 1J 27
Quarry Rd. TN1: Tun W 4K 33
Queens Ct. TN12: Pad W 7J 25
Queens Dr. TN14: S'oaks 5J 3
Queen's Gdns. TN4: Tun W 3K 33
Queen's Rd. TN4: Tun W 4J 33
QUEEN STREET 7K 25
Queen St. TN12: Pad W 3J 31
Queripel Cl. TN2: Tun W 3A 34
Quincewood Gdns. TN10: Tonb 7K 17

R

Raeburn Cl. TN10: Tonb 1C 22
Ragge Way TN15: Seal 5B 4
Railway App. TN9: Tonb 6K 21
Railway Ho. TN1: Tun W 4K 33

RAMSLYE 1F 37
Ramslye Rd. TN4: Tun W 1F 37
Randall Hill Rd. TN15: Wro 1D 6
Rankine Rd. TN2: Tun W 2B 34
Raphael Ct. TN11: Hild 7F 17
Raptor Centre, The 4C 36
Ravenswood Av. TN2: Tun W 3A 34
Rear, The TN2: Tun W 6A 40
(off The Pantiles)
Rectory Dr. TN3: Bidb 5E 26
Rectory La. TN13: S'oaks 4J 9
TN15: Igh .7A 6
Red Ho. Cotts. TN13: S'oaks 3J 9
Redland Av. TN4: R'hall 5E 32
Redlands Rd. TN13: S'oaks 2F 9
Redleaf Cl. TN2: Tun W 3B 34
Redmans Pl. TN13: S'oaks 3J 9
(off Akehurst La.)
Redpoll Wlk. TN12: Pad W 3G 31
Red Roses Cl. TN12: E Peck 1F 25
Redwell Cotts. TN15: Igh 1A 12
Redwell La. TN15: Igh 1K 11
Redwings La. TN2: Pem 7H 29
Redwood Pk. TN12: Cap 3A 30
Reeds La. TN11: S'brne 1C 18
Regency Hall TN2: Tun W 6A 40 (7J 33)
Regency Ho. TN2: Tun W 5D 40
Regent Pl. TN2: Tun W 6B 34
Regina Ct. TN4: Tun W 5H 33
Registry Office
Tunbridge Wells 4D 40 (6K 33)
Rembrandt Cl. TN10: Tonb 1C 22
Retreat, The TN13: S'oaks 3H 9
Reynolds Cl. TN10: Tonb 1C 22
Reynolds La. TN4: Tun W 2H 33
Ribston Cl. TN15: Wro 1E 30
Richard Beau Nash Apartments
TN1: Tun W 1D 40 (5K 33)
Richardson Rd. TN4: Tun W 3J 33
Richmond Pl. TN2: Tun W 1K 37
Riddlesdale Av. TN4: Tun W 3J 33
Ridge, The TN3: Groom 6A 36
Ridgelands TN3: Bidb 4E 26
Ridgeway TN2: Pem 2H 35
Ridgeway, The TN10: Tonb 2A 22
Ridgeway Cres. TN10: Tonb 3B 22
Ridgewaye, The TN4: S'bgh 7J 27
Ridgy Fld. Cl. TN15: Wro 2E 6
Riding La. TN11: Hild 1F 21
Riding Pk. TN11: Hild 7F 17
Ridings, The TN2: Tun W 3D 34
TN12: Pad W 1G 31
Riggs Way TN15: Wro 1D 6
Ringden Av. TN12: Pad W 3E 30
Rings Hill TN11: Hild 1D 20
Rise, The TN13: S'oaks 7J 9
River Ct. TN13: Riv 7E 2
Riverdale Est. TN9: Tonb 7B 22
RIVERHEAD 7E 2
Riverhead M. TN13: Riv 1E 8
RIVER HILL .1A 16
Riverhill TN13: S'oaks 1K 15
Riverhill Himalayan Gdns. 2A 16
River Lawn Rd. TN9: Tonb 6K 21
River Pde. TN13: Riv 7E 2
Riverside Ct. TN9: Tonb 6A 22
Riverside Retail Pk. TN14: S'oaks . . .4J 3
River Wlk. TN9: Tonb 6K 21
Robinwood Dr. TN15: Seal 4B 4
Robyns Way TN13: S'oaks 7F 3
Rochdale Rd. TN1: Tun W 4A 34
Rochester Rd. TN10: Tonb 3B 22
Rockdale TN13: S'oaks 3H 9
Rockdale Gdns. TN13: S'oaks 3H 9
Rockdale Pleasance TN13: S'oaks 4H 9
Rockdale Rd. TN13: S'oaks 3J 9
Rock Hill TN15: Bor G 5D 6
Rock Villa Rd. TN1: Tun W . . .2B 40 (5J 33)
Rodmell Rd. TN2: Tun W 6B 40 (7J 33)
Rodney Av. TN10: Tonb 3C 22

Roedean Hgts. TN2: Tun W 7B 40 (1J 37)	St Barnabas Cl. TN1: Tun W 4K 33
Roedean Rd. TN2: Tun W 7B 40 (1J 37)	St Bernards Rd. TN10: Tonb 1A 22
Rogues Hill TN11: Pens 2B 26	St Botolph's Av. TN15: S'oaks 2G 9
Roma Ct. TN13: S'oaks 6H 3	St Botolph's Rd. TN13: S'oaks 2H 9
Roman Ct. TN15: Bor G 5D 6	St Clere TN15: Kems'g 1H 5
ROMFORD .2K 35	St David's Rd. TN4: Tun W 3K 33
Romford Rd. TN2: Pem . . . . .2H 35 & 7B 30	St Eanswythe's Ct. TN9: Tonb 7A 22
Romney Way TN10: Tonb 2C 22	St Edith Cotts. TN15: Kems'g 1K 5
Ronley Ct. *TN13: S'oaks* 6J 3	St Edith's Farm Cott. TN15: Kems'g . . .3D 4
(off Hillingdon Av.)	St Edith's Rd. TN15: Kems'g 3C 4
Rookdean TN13: Chip 7C 2	St Georges Ct. *TN4: Tun W* 4J 33
Rookley Cl. TN2: Tun W 7B 34	*(off Queens Rd.)*
Rooks Hill TN15: Under 7E 10	TN15: Wro 1D 6
Roopers TN3: Speld 2C 32	St George's M. TN9: Tonb 7K 21
Roper's Ga. TN4: Tun W 1G 37	St George's Pk. TN2: Tun W 2H 37
Rosecroft Pk. TN3: Lang G 5C 32	St George's Rd. TN13: S'oaks 7H 3
Rosefield TN13: S'oaks 2G 9	St Hildas TN15: Plax 5D 12
Rosehill Wlk. TN1: Tun W . . .3A 40 (6J 33)	St James Cl. TN10: Tonb 7B 18
Rosemary Pl. TN12: Pad W 7G 25	St James Ct. TN1: Tun W . . .1D 40 (5K 33)
Rose St. TN9: Tonb 7A 22	St James' Pk. TN1: Tun W 4A 34
Rossdale TN2: Tun W 4B 34	St James' Rd. TN1: Tun W . . .1E 40 (4K 33)
Rother Rd. TN10: Tonb 2K 21	St James's Rd. TN13: S'oaks 7H 3
ROUGHWAY 7F 13	ST JOHN'S
Roughway La.	TN4 . . . . .4J 33
TN11: S'brne, Dunk G 7E 12	TN13 . . . . .7J 3
Roundhill Rd. TN2: Tun W 1B 38	St Johns Cl. TN4: Tun W 4J 33
Rowan Cl. TN12: Pad W 3F 31	St John's Ct. TN13: S'oaks 7J 3
Rowan M. TN10: Tonb 3A 22	St John's Hill TN13: S'oaks 6J 3
Rowan Shaw TN10: Tonb 1B 22	St John's Pk. TN4: Tun W 1J 33
Rowan Tree Rd. TN2: Tun W 1G 37	St John's Rd.
Row Dow TN14: Otf 1K 3	TN4: S'bgh, Tun W 1B 40 (1J 33)
Rowley Hill TN2: Pem 7H 29	TN13: S'oaks 6H 3
Royal Av. TN9: Tonb 7A 22	St Julian Rd. TN15: S'oaks, Under 1K 15
Royal Chase TN4: Tun W 1A 40 (4H 33)	St Lawrence Av. TN4: Bidb 5F 27
Royal Ri. TN9: Tonb 7A 22	St Luke's Rd. TN4: Tun W 3K 33
Royal Spa Retail Pk. TN2: Tun W 7C 28	St Mark's Rd. TN2: Tun W 2H 37
ROYAL TUNBRIDGE WELLS	St Marys Cl. ME18: Ladd 3K 25
. . . . .5A 40 (7J 33)	TN15: Platt 5G 7
Royal Tunbridge Wells Bus. Pk.	St Mary's Dr. TN13: Riv 1E 8
TN2: Tun W 7C 28	St Mary's La. TN3: Speld 1C 32
Royal Tunbridge Wells District	ST MARYS PLATT 5G 7
Indoor Bowls Club, The 7C 34	St Mary's Rd. TN15: Platt, Wro H 1K 27
Royal Victoria Hall 7J 27	TN15: Wro 2E 6
Royal Victoria Pl.	St Michaels Ct. TN11: Hild 7F 17
TN1: Tun W 1C 40 (5K 33)	St Michael's Dr. TN14: Otf 1K 3
Royal W. Kent Av. TN10: Tonb 3B 22	St Michael's Rd. TN4: Tun W 2K 33
Ruscombe Cl. TN4: S'bgh 6H 27	St Nicholas Ct. *TN13: S'oaks* 3H 9
Rushetts TN3: Lang G 5B 32	*(off Lime Tree Wlk.)*
Rushlye Cl. TN3: Bell G 5D 38	St Nicholas Dr. TN13: S'oaks 4H 9
Rushmere Ct. TN15: Igh 5B 6	St Paul's Cl. TN10: Tonb 2B 22
Rushymead TN15: Kems'g 3C 4	St Pauls Ct. TN4: R'hall 5E 32
Russell M. TN12: Pad W 1F 31	St Paul's St. TN4: R'hall 5E 32
Russett Rd. TN12: E Peck 1F 25	St Peters St. TN4: Tun W 6A 34
RUSTHALL .5E 32	St Philips Ct. TN2: Tun W 3B 34
Rusthall Grange TN4: R'hall 5F 33	St Stephens Ct. TN1: Tun W 4K 33
Rusthall Pk. TN4: R'hall, Tun W 5F 33	St Stephen's St. TN9: Tonb 7K 21
Rusthall Pl. TN4: R'hall 6F 33	St Vincent's La. ME19: Addtn 3K 7
Rusthall Rd. TN4: R'hall 5E 32	Salisbury Cl. TN10: Tonb 2B 22
Rustwick TN4: R'hall 5F 33	Salisbury Rd. TN3: Lang G 6B 32
Rutherford Way TN10: Tonb 7B 18	TN4: Tun W 1A 34
Rycroft La. TN15: S'oaks 1E 14	TN10: Tonb 3B 22
Rydal Cl. TN4: Tun W 4G 33	Salmans La. TN11: Pens 2A 26
Rydal Dr. TN4: Tun W 4G 33	Salomons Mus.
Ryders TN3: Lang G 6C 32	(Canterbury Christ Church University)
Ryecroft Rd. TN14: Otf 2G 3	. . . . .1F 33
Rye La. TN14: Dun G, Otf 5F 3	Salomons Rd. TN4: R'hall 5E 32
Rye Lane Pottery 5F 3	Sanderson Way TN9: Tonb 6B 22
Ryewood Cotts. TN14: Dun G 5F 3	Sandhurst Av. TN2: Pem 3J 35
Rymers Cl. TN2: Tun W 2B 34	Sandhurst Cl. TN2: Tun W 2A 34
	Sandhurst Pk. TN2: Tun W 2A 34
	Sandhurst Rd. TN2: Tun W 2A 34
S	Sandilands TN13: Chip 7D 2
	Sandown Cl. TN2: Tun W 3D 34
Sackville Cl. TN13: S'oaks 7H 3	Sandown Gro. TN2: Tun W 3D 34
St Andrew's Cl. TN12: Pad W 2G 31	SANDOWN PARK 3D 34
St Andrews Ct. TN4: S'bgh 7J 27	Sandown Pk. TN2: Tun W 4D 34
St Andrew's Pk. Rd. TN4: S'bgh 7J 27	Sandringham M. TN4: Tun W 4J 33
St Andrew's Rd. TN12: Pad W 2G 31	Sandrock Ho. TN2: Tun W 5B 34
St Augustine Ho. *TN9: Tonb* 7K 21	Sandrock Rd.
(off Priory Rd.)	TN2: Tun W 1E 40 (5A 34)

Sandy La. ME19: Addtn 3K 7
TN13: S'oaks 1J 9
TN15: Igh, Ivy H 3K 11
TN15: Wro H 3K 7
Sandy Ridge TN15: Bor G 5E 6
Saunders Rd. TN4: Tun W 1G 37
Saville Cl. TN10: Tonb 7B 18
Saxbys Rd. TN15: Seal 7F 5
Saxby Wood TN11: Leigh 6B 20
Saxon Cl. TN14: Otf 2F 3
Saxon Ho. TN14: S'oaks 6K 3
Scabharbour Rd. TN11: Hild 7J 15
TN14: Hild, Weald 4J 15
School App. TN15: Bor G 5E 6
School La. TN11: Hdlw 5J 19
TN11: Plax, S'brne 6C 12
TN15: Plax 6C 12
TN15: Seal 6B 4
School Ri. TN2: Tun W 1H 37
Scott Rd. TN9: Tonb 7H 21
Scotts Way TN2: Tun W 2G 37
TN13: Riv 7E 2
Seabrook Rd. TN10: Tonb 3J 21
SEAL 6B 4
SEAL CHART 1E 10
Sealcroft Cotts. TN15: Seal 4B 4
Seal Dr. TN15: Seal 6B 4
Seal Hollow Rd. TN13: S'oaks 2J 9
TN15: S'oaks 2J 9
Seal Rd. TN14: S'oaks 6J 3
TN15: S'oaks 6J 3
Sebastopol La. TN12: Five G 7D 24
Selby's Cotts. TN11: Hild 3F 21
Sellbourne Pk. TN3: Frant 6A 38
Senlac Pl. *TN3: Groom* 5C 36
(off Meadow Rd.)
Sennocke Ct. TN13: S'oaks 3H 9
Serpentine Ct. TN13: S'oaks 7K 3
Serpentine Rd. TN13: S'oaks 1J 9
Seven Mile La.
TN15: Platt, Wro H 4K 7
SEVENOAKS 3J 9
Sevenoaks Bus. Cen.
TN14: S'oaks 6J 3
Sevenoaks By-Pass
TN14: Ide H, S'oaks, Sund, Weald
. . . . .1C 8
SEVENOAKS COMMON 6H 9
SEVENOAKS HOSPITAL 6J 3
Sevenoaks Leisure Cen. 3J 9
Sevenoaks Mus. & Art Gallery 3J 9
Sevenoaks Rd. TN14: Otf, S'oaks 1H 3
TN15: Bor G 5C 6
TN15: Igh, Seal 1H 11
Sevenoaks Station (Rail) 2G 9
SEVENOAKS WEALD 4H 15
Sevenoaks Wildlife Reserve 6F 3
Severn Cl. TN10: Tonb 2A 22
Shab Hall Cotts. TN13: Dun G 3C 2
Shaftesbury Rd. TN4: Tun W 3J 33
Shakespeare Rd. TN9: Tonb 7H 21
Shambles, The TN13: S'oaks 3J 9
Shandon Cl. TN2: Tun W 5A 34
Shaw, The TN2: Tun W 7A 34
SHEET HILL 3D 12
Sheet Hill TN15: Plax 3B 12
Sheffield Rd. TN4: S'bgh 6H 27
Sheilings, The TN15: Seal 5B 4
Shelton Cl. TN10: Tonb 2A 22
Shenden Cl. TN13: S'oaks 5J 9
Shenden Way TN13: S'oaks 6J 9
Shepherds Wlk. TN2: Tun W 5B 34
Sherborne Cl. TN2: Tun W 7B 34
Sherborne Gro. TN15: Kems'g 2C 4
Sherbourne Pl. TN2: Tun W 7A 40
Sherenden Pk. TN11: Gold G 2A 24
(not continuous)
Sherenden Rd. TN11: Tude 6G 23
Sheridan Ct. TN11: Hild 3H 21
Shernfold Pk. TN3: Frant 7A 38

Y

Z

SAFETY CAMERA INFORMATION

PocketGPSWorld.com's CamerAlert is a self-contained speed and red light camera warning system for SatNavs and Android or Apple iOS smartphones/tablets. Visit www.cameralert.co.uk to download.

Safety camera locations are publicised by the Safer Roads Partnership which operates them in order to encourage drivers to comply with speed limits at these sites. It is the driver's absolute responsibility to be aware of and to adhere to speed limits at all times.

By showing this safety camera information it is the intention of Geographers' A-Z Map Company Ltd., to encourage safe driving and greater awareness of speed limits and vehicle speed. Data accurate at time of printing.

Discover over 300 A-Z maps and atlases

Key to Maps

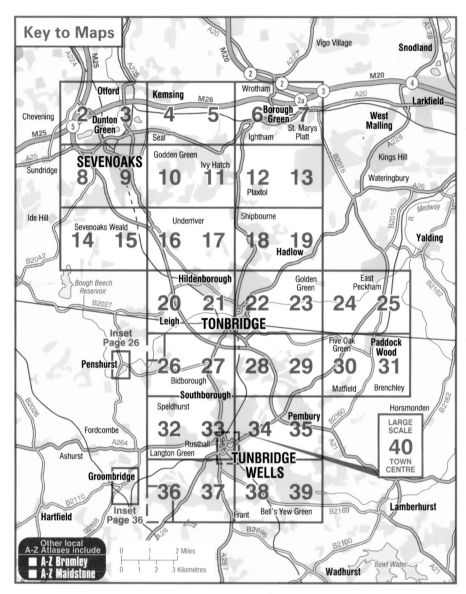

Vigo Village · Snodland · Larkfield · West Malling · Kings Hill · Wateringbury · Yalding · Lamberhurst · Wadhurst

Otford · **Kemsing** · Wrotham · **Borough Green** · St. Marys Platt

2 **3** **4** **5** **6** **7**

Chevening · **Dunton Green** · Seal · Ightham

SEVENOAKS · Godden Green · Ivy Hatch · Plaxtol

8 **9** **10** **11** **12** **13**

Sundridge · Ide Hill

Sevenoaks Weald · Underriver · Shipbourne · **Hadlow**

14 **15** **16** **17** **18** **19**

Bough Beech Reservoir · **Hildenborough** · Golden Green · East Peckham

20 **21** **22** **23** **24** **25**

Leigh · **TONBRIDGE**

Inset Page 26

Penshurst · Bidborough · Five Oak Green · **Paddock Wood** · Matfield · Brenchley

26 **27** **28** **29** **30** **31**

Southborough · Speldhurst · **Pembury** · Horsmonden

Fordcombe · Rusthall · Langton Green

32 **33** **34** **35**

LARGE SCALE 40 TOWN CENTRE

Ashurst · **TUNBRIDGE WELLS**

Groombridge

Inset Page 36 · Frant · Bell's Yew Green

Hartfield

36 **37** **38** **39**

Lamberhurst

Bewl Water · **Wadhurst**

Other local A-Z Atlases include
- A-Z Bromley
- A-Z Maidstone

0   1   2 Miles
0   1   2   3 Kilometres

Geographers' A-Z Map Company Ltd
Fairfield Road, Borough Green,
Sevenoaks, Kent TN15 8PP
Enquiries & Trade Sales
01732 781000
Retail Sales
01732 783422

ISBN 978-1-84348-849-1

£4.95

PORTSMOUTH

Including FAREHAM, GOSPORT, HAVANT, HORNDEAN

Clanfield, Cosham, Cowplain, Emsworth, Denmead
Hayling Island, Lee-on-the-Solent, Portchester
Southwick, Waterlooville, Westbourne, Wickham

PORTSMOUTH **CITY CENTRE** LARGE SCALE

INDEX INCLUDES

- **OVER 6,500 STREETS**
- **INDUSTRIAL ESTATES**
- **SUBSIDIARY ADDRESSES**

FOR AREA COVERED SEE MAPS INSIDE

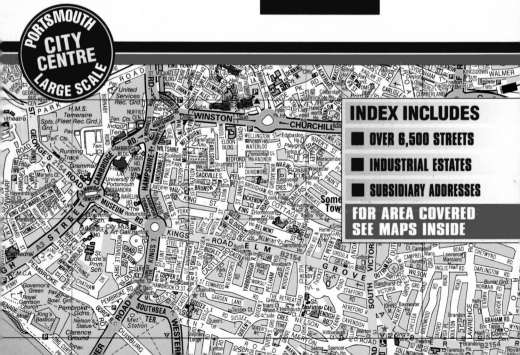

Paperback 15 1/2"x10 1/2" 4 miles to 1inch

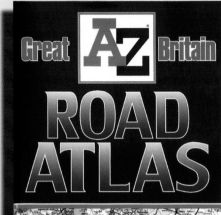

Great Britain
Road Atlases

Spiralbound 11"x15" 2 1/2 miles to 1inch

Casebound 7 3/4"x11" 3 1/2 miles to 1inch

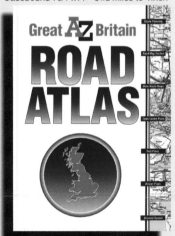

Have you got the latest edition?